HOW TO CREATE A LIFE OF UNFORGETTABLE IMPACT & ABUNDANT FULFILLMENT

PRESENTED BY
RYAN C. GREENE

MAKE IT MATTER!
How To Create A Life Of Unforgettable Impact & Abundant Fulfillment

www.ryancgreene.com

Cover design by: GreeneHouse Media, Print Division

ISBN: 978-1-7364175-0-8
Printed in the USA

Published by
GreeneHouse Media

DEDICATION

This book is dedicated to my father, the late Rev. Dr. Harry A. Greene. My only wish is that you were still here to see this and cheer me on. I love you and miss you immensely. Thank you for everything you were, are and forever will be to me.

ACKNOWLEDGEMENTS

Let me first thank every author and contributor on this amazing project. **Make It Matter!** would not have had nearly the impact it's going to have, had you not shared your gift with us through this project. Thank you for allowing me to stretch your comfort zone as we "dreamed the impossible dream" on this project and made it come true.

Thank you so much to our two editors, Rev. Stephanie Jenkins and Moné Moore. Your professionalism and thorough work proved essential in helping us present our stories in the best light. I'm forever grateful to your husband and mom, respectively, for referring you when I put out the call.

Thank you, Dr. Cheryl Wood, for always answering my call. Your contribution to this project was invaluable and I so appreciate all you do and bring to the table. I wish this industry were full of more people with your spirit.

Thank you to Brian J. Olds and the Black Speakers Network. The amazing platform you have built has been invaluable to so many Black speakers. Thank you for your contribution and co-sign on this project.

I want to acknowledge you, the reader. Don't take this moment in time lightly. We have all been given a once in a generation opportunity to reset our direction in life and make the impact we were purposed to make while living the fulfilled life we were also purposed to live. Use it wisely and make it matter.

Last, but certainly not least, I want to acknowledge my wife, Tyneka. If being stuck in the house together every day for over a year taught me nothing else, it taught me that I chose the right one. I love you as my wife and cherish you as my friend. Thank you for your constant support and love.

TABLE OF CONTENTS

INTRODUCTION

CREATING A LIFE OF UNFORGETTABLE IMPACT & ABUNDANT FULFILLMENT

What does it truly mean to live life? If recent times have forced us to do anything, it's forced us to re-evaluate two things about ourselves; the impact our decisions have in on our lives, and the fulfillment they bring to us and others.

As society struggles to define its "new normal", the reality has hit many that "normal" is no longer an acceptable benchmark. People are looking at their lives and asking the same question, "Does any of this really matter?"

For many, this year has been like Toto pulling back the curtain on the Wizard of Oz and exposing everything we once drove ourselves crazy over believing it validated us and made us feel accomplished, as just smoke and mirrors.

Most people were sold the same bill of goods for what makes a successful life. Get a good education, get a good job, work hard until you can retire at 67, then go enjoy the rest of the life you have left. But is that it? Is that all our lives are supposed to be? If it all ended today, can you definitively say you lived your most impactful and fulfilled life

Too many people have fallen into the trap of simply existing and going about their lives doing what they do, simply because that's what they've always done. Never providing lasting impact in their space and never experiencing true fulfillment from their work.

THAT. STOPS. TODAY.

This book is designed to make sure you never again feel like all you've worked so hard to achieve doesn't even matter. After reading this book, you will know exactly how to look at different areas of your life, decide what matters and what doesn't, and know how to create a more impactful and fulfilling life for yourself and others.

The featured authors will cover how to make your story matter, your business matter, your money matter, your relationships matter, your legacy matter, your work matter, and so much more. This book promises to help you quit blindly going through life to check off boxes as accomplishments that don't truly resonate to what matters for YOU.

You will be able to look at your life, overcome your fears of how others may judge your decisions, and unapologetically pursue life on your own terms. Reality hit most of us in 2020 when we learned how little so much of what we thought mattered really matters in making our life impactful and fulfilling. Many of us have packed our lives with frivolous activities or simple beliefs that meet someone else's definition of success but bring no substantial value to our own lives.

Writing this book was a labor of love, but only the first step. After you read the book, be sure to enroll in the companion online masterclass. The masterclass is where transformation happens on an even deeper level. The masterclass is loaded with video trainings from each featured author, special **MAKE IT MATTER**! Moment spotlight interviews, additional trainings, audios, videos, and resources that are constantly being added to assist in your journey. Scan the QR code below with your cell phone camera for instant access and use the promo code MATTER for a special discount.

As if the book and masterclass weren't enough, there's also the **Make It Matter**! Movie! The movie will be an adaptation of the principles outlined in the book in a comedic feature film. Those enrolled in the masterclass will get premium first-look access to the film when it's released.

As you can see, this project is bigger than these pages in your hand or on your screen. Our goal is to reach 1,000,000 people and help them change just one thing in their lives that will help them create unforgettable impact and have abundant fulfillment. You can help us in that goal by doing a few things:

1. Be sure to tell everyone about the book on Facebook and Instagram and tell them to purchase a copy. Make sure you tag *@themakeitmatterproject.*
2. Enroll in the masterclass for the full **MAKE IT MATTER**! experience
3. Share a review of the book on Amazon.com
4. Subscribe to the **MAKE IT MATTER**! podcast on your favorite podcast provider
5. Watch the movie when it's released and spread good words about it online
6. Ask your boss, church, club or organization, to order a case of books for your group!

This is your time to live the life you've always dreamed of living. It's time for you to **MAKE IT MATTER!**

RYAN C.
GREENE

Whether via a stage in front of thousands, over the radio and television airwaves, or through one of his many bestselling books, "The Passionpreneur" Ryan C. Greene serves as a strategic marketing coach to speakers, content experts, and authors. Ryan uses his story and experience to empower audiences with the knowledge and practical training to grow as leaders while maximizing their impact and creating lives of abundant fulfilment.

Having shared stages with speaking greats like Dr. Willie Jolley, Delatorro McNeal II, Dr. Cheryl Wood, and George Fraser, Ryan is one of the nation's most sought after trainers on impact leadership, personal & professional development, and strategic marketing.

Ryan C. Greene is an entrepreneur, author coach, bestselling author, and professional speaker. He is the Founder of GreeneHouse Media LLC, a media company whose goal is to provide "Media With A Purpose" via radio, television, film, and books. Ryan is the author of ten books, hosts and executive produces several podcasts and web shows, and founded Indie Author PRO, an author development company specializing in teaching authors how to monetize their content, automate their business and become top-revenue authors.

CONTACT:

Book Ryan for interviews or to speak: *www.ryancgreene.com*

Work with Ryan on your book: *www.indieauthorpro.com*

Facebook/Instagram/Twitter/LinkedIn/YouTube: *@rygspeaks*

Email: ryan@ryancgreene.com

Text PASSION to (614) 333-0338 for a FREE GIFT to learn how to monetize your expertise and start getting paid for what you know.

MAKE IT

There I was working a job I hated. A job I felt was literally sucking the life out of me every single time I walked into the place. Each morning it was the same routine. I would sit in the parking lot and think of all the other ways I could be spending the next eight hours instead of being tied to that desk and phone. About five minutes before I was due to clock-in, I'd walk towards the employee entrance and up the stairs to the third floor. Once I would get to the third floor, I would look over rail to the first floor below and ponder the same question, "If I jumped, would this fall kill me?" After deciding not to jump, I would say "Good morning" to the one or two co-workers I actually liked, then rush to my cubicle just in time to clock in before my shift started.

To be clear, I wasn't suicidal. "The Passionpreneur" would never kill himself. But that situation made me feel like I was committing suicide to my purpose, passions, and potential. Looking over that rail each morning served as my visual representation of sorts to remind me just what I was allowing to happen in my life. Each day I questioned, "Is this going to be the day I get fed up and quit, or is this the day they are finally going to fire me?" I was underpaid, underappreciated, and undervalued. I had forgotten more experience and knowledge than my bosses had ever possessed. I knew my life right then looked nothing like the life I dreamed of for myself when I was young and felt invincible. I was stuck in a position where I knew I didn't matter. All the books I had written didn't matter. All the stages I had spoken on didn't matter. All my experience and education didn't matter. Yet, there I was. Allowing it all to happen as I did what I had to do to get by, because we all know "these bills ain't gonna pay themselves."

Eventually, when it came time to renew my employment contract, management decided not to renew me, and my employment ended. Technically, I didn't quit, and they didn't fire me. I guess neither one of us wanted to be the first to say, "Goodbye." We just went our separate ways. While having to tell my wife that my job let me go was the difficult part, I must

The place where hopes and dreams go to die.

admit, I was more relieved and excited about it than I had been about anything in a long time. No, I didn't have something else lined up. No, I didn't have six-months to a year's salary saved up. All I had was a resolve to make sure I was never in that situation again. A resolve that, with all the talent and know-how I possessed, I would never again sell myself short simply because I needed a paycheck. I knew too much to be that guy again. I declared that day that no matter what I did going forward, I wanted my work to matter.

So, this is a story all about how my life got flipped, turned upside down. No, wait. That story's already been told. This story is about my journey to making my life matter. I believe everyone's life matters. The fact that we're alive matters. But there were two major elements I felt were missing from my life. I had accomplished so much, overcome so much, and yet there I was struggling once again to put it all together. I realized I was missing two things.

First, I realized I needed everything I put my time and energy into to have an unforgettable impact on the lives of those I touch. Not some average, run of the mill, forgettable impact. I want my impact to be so tremendous that it is impossible to replace the mark I made. I don't want people to ever replace or forget the impact I made on the job in front of me! Secondly, and of equal importance, I needed to experience abundant fulfillment from my work. Oh yeah, no more sacrificing my joy simply because I need money. Helping people didn't have to be a thankless job that enriched everyone else but me. If I am going to work on something, I am going to love it. Let me tell you something. When I began saying "No" to paying gigs and jobs because I knew I wasn't going to enjoy doing that work, there was a peace that filled me like I've never felt. That decision also helped me streamline my product/service offerings as well as focus on my ideal client. That focus led to more success and joy in the past three years than I felt in the first thirteen years of business combined.

Once I decided to make it matter and create a life of unforgettable impact and abundant fulfillment, I experienced life in a much more vibrant way. It was as if I were trying to live a 4K life in a 720p world to that point. So, like I have done with my 6 previous books, once I live it and practice it myself, I then write about it to teach you. If I've done nothing over my 15 years career as an author and speaker, I have stressed the importance of living a fearless, purposeful life on your terms while chasing your passions and breaking free of your reliance on a company to dictate and control your worth and value. For many, it took the global pandemic and shutdown we all experienced to show them just how fragile their security and success truly was. The year 2020 exposed to everyone the things in our lives that really matter and what things were all a façade used to placate us as we blindly ran the hamster wheel of the American Dream.

This **MAKE IT MATTER!** project serves one purpose. That purpose is to provide the tools you need to create your own life of unforgettable impact and abundant fulfillment. When the idea for this book first came to me, the plan was for me to write the entire book myself. Then it hit me. In a book about creating greater impact, one simple way to do that would be by inviting others to join me in the book to share their voices. So that's what I did. I have assembled this collection of authors for this book, interviewed numerous top-performing industry leaders, created an online masterclass, and even wrote and directed a feature film all to create an experience that walks you through the journey of making your life matter in every way possible. Each professional spotlighted in this project is a specialist in their area and is ready to serve you.

I want you to enjoy your journey and achieve milestones you once thought were out of reach. If you are reading this book, then it is time to celebrate. You made it! You survived the darkest time our country has seen in many of our lifetimes. You are not still here by accident. 2020 was your chance to hit the reset button and take inventory of your life thus far. It was your opportunity to determine if you are satisfied with the status quo, or ready to make some significant changes. Have you been living an authentic life that provides true fulfillment for yourself, or have you been trying to satisfy the outside expectations of others? Have you made the type of lasting impact on your family, career, and community that you hoped to, or have you just been doing enough to get by each day?

So let's get into it. I How do we make our lives matter? What should we focus on to help create a more impactful and fulfilling life? Some may be more fun than others, but they are important. Whichever one hurts the most or hits the hardest to you, start there! No more playing it safe and comfortable. What has always been does not have to always be, if you decide it shouldn't be. If you're ready to make it matter, let's go!

MAKE YOUR STORY MATTER

"Story over stats. What makes you who you are is not the boxes you check, but the impact of your story."
~ Inspired by Michelle Obama

This is my tenth book I've written since I released my first book, Success Is In Your Hand, back in January 2005. When I wrote that first book, it was purely as a companion to my first signature talk as a new motivational speaker. Before writing books, my passion was songwriting. Back in the mid-to-late 90's, I had a dream of becoming a big-time songwriter like Babyface. My only issue (and by only, I mean the biggest issue ever), was that while I was a fantastic songwriter, I was not a great singer, nor could I play any instruments. That made recording my demo songs darn near impossible. All I was left with from that dream was a binder full of lyrics the world never got to hear.

Fast forward to 2005 and the release of my first book. One thing I learned while pursuing a songwriting career was that publishing was kind. When I decided to write my first book, I knew right away that I had to own my publishing. Ever the entrepreneur, I never wanted to sign with a book publisher. I wanted to be the book publisher. So that's what I did. I started my company, Bakari Book Publishers, and began publishing my books, as well as those of other authors. Sidenote: here's a tip. Pick a company name people can pronounce. I wanted a company name that mattered. While "Bakari" was dope to me because it meant "one with great promise," everyone continually mispronounced it! I can't tell you how many times while being introduced to speak, I would hear people say I was the founder of "Bacardi Books". So, eventually I changed the name to GreeneHouse Media.

When I changed my company name to GreeneHouse Media, I added the slogan "Media That Matters". This was in 2008. Even back then, I was determined to only publish books that had some redeeming quality to them that uplifted and empowered people. This was at the height of the rise of urban street literature, so while seemingly every Black author was releasing books with covers that looked like a No Limit Records album cover, and content that would even make Zane clutch her pearls, I was committed to producing uplifting personal development books that spoke to people on their level by using my life experiences without being preachy.

In the past 16 years, I have made an impact by literally making my story matter. I built an entire company and brand off the crazy notion that my story was powerful and relatable enough to change the lives of those who were open to hearing it and willing to put in the work for themselves. I believe everyone has their story to tell. In my last book, Becoming A Passionpreneur®, I teach you how to monetize your expertise. The final step in my system is to "Live your story. Tell your story." There is power in your story. Each of us has lived a life full of experiences that have taught us something and made us wiser. Taught us things that someone else would find valuable-if only we weren't afraid to share our story with them.

Your story can only have impact on others when you overcome your fear of embarrassment and shame and decide to tell it. When I started sharing my story, over and over people would tell me they were experiencing the same issues I was, but they thought they were all alone. Or, they had been struggling to achieve certain breakthroughs for years, but the answer finally clicked for them once they read my story. When I first set out to be an author, my goal was to always make it about the message, and not about the messenger. My focus was to speak to people where they were, as someone who is more like them than not. I never wanted to be one of those "experts" who felt that being able to woo audiences by speaking over their heads and trying to be so faux-deep is what made them impactful. Sure, I could scrawl scripts of capacious resplendent colloquy, but why do that when simply saying "I could write books with big fancy words" get the job done and creates greater impact? The only way to make your story matter, is if those to whom you're telling the story can understand what the heck you're talking about.

After 16 years in book publishing, 10 books written, hundreds of author clients served, and over 100 Amazon Bestseller Lists reached, I knew it was time to shift to the next phase of my career in this industry by helping others make their stories matter. Now, as the Founder of Indie Author PRO, I coach current and aspiring authors on how to strategically tell their stories and market their books so they can make their stories matter. Telling your story is one thing; but telling it in a way that creates unforgettable impact for readers and moves them to action is what separates unknown writers from top-earning authors. If telling your story is on your bucket list, be sure to visit www.IndieAuthorPRO.com to see how we can serve you.

MAKE YOUR PAIN AND SETBACKS MATTER

"I'd rather regret the risks that didn't work out than the chances I didn't take at all."
~ Simone Biles

In 2018, Stacey Abrams and Andrew Gillum both lost tight gubernatorial elections in Georgia and Florida, respectively. Both were initially longshots to win as Black candidates in their southern states, but as the campaign seasons trudged on, they both began making headway and eventually became legitimate contenders. In the end, thanks to good old voter suppression and under-handed tactics by their Republican opponents, both ended up losing their contests. In the two years since their loss, Andrew Gillum's reputation took a major hit, and his ascending career came to a screeching halt. According to Gillum, he "turned to alcohol" to overcome the pain of his defeat and was found naked and clinging to life in a hotel room as a result of an apparent accidental drug overdose.

How did Stacey Abrams deal with her defeat that was literally stolen from her? The short answer is she very literally saved our entire country and democracy as we know it. Stacey spent the next two years doubling down on her efforts to fight voter suppression in Georgia. Through her Fair Fight organization, she organized and led efforts to demand the voices of those who were silenced and cheated in 2018 be heard in 2020. Instead of sulking in her pain and having pity parties for herself, she committed her work to ensuring no other Georgian candidate would feel the pain she felt from having an election stolen from them, and no other voter would have the voice silenced. Her tireless work and leadership have now turned the southern stronghold state of Georgia blue and delivered not only a win for President Joe Biden, but also sent two Democratic Senators to Washington, DC. That's how you make your pain and setbacks matter!

When you are hit with a setback, you have two choices:

Transform that experience into a positive, or let the momentary failure destroy you. Failure is only forever if you allow it to be. You have the power to set the expiration date on your failure. The moment you decide to get back up, your failure becomes a success story. All it takes is you evaluating the situation, assessing your options, and deciding to pick up the pieces and press forward. No great accomplishment has ever been achieved on the first try. Steve Jobs was fired from the company he created before being re-hired by Apple and making it the juggernaut it is today. Michael Jordan, the greatest basketball player ever, was cut from his high school hoops team. Both J.K. Rowling and Tyler Perry were broke and on welfare before their stories became billion-dollar brands in literature, theater, and film. Even Colonel Sanders' secret recipe was rejected over one thousand times before one restaurant finally accepted it, and that chicken is delicious!

No one enjoys failure or pain. Like it or not, it's a fact of life that we will all experience setbacks on some level. If you aren't failing, it's only because you aren't trying. The key is to plan for the setbacks and be prepared to use them to catapult you to greater success. While you may be the one going through the setbacks firsthand, they aren't solely for you. Look at your setbacks as your gifts from the greatest teacher we all know: Experience. Whenever you face setbacks, it's important to ask yourself, "What lessons in this experience are for my personal growth, and what lessons are for me to use to impact the lives of others?"

Dr. Willie Jolley is probably most well-known for his quote, "Your setback is a setup for a comeback." That's only true for those who don't want their story to end with them in their proverbial hotel room, naked and overdosed. I don't want to minimize the anyone's actual pain and setbacks, but I want to see you make your pain your bit-- Whoa! I got a little too hype there. Let me calm down. All I'm saying is, your setbacks are the beginnings of your success, not the end. You have the power, and dare I say, the permission, to make your pain and setbacks matter, if you choose.

MAKE YOUR TIME AND PRESENCE MATTER

"The greatest mistake we make in life is thinking we have time."
~ Kobe Bryant

Can I talk about my father for a few paragraphs? This book is dedicated to him, but I want to do something I've never done in my previous books, and that is talk about our relationship. My father, Rev. Dr. Harry A. Greene passed away on September 9, 2020. It was sudden and unexpected, and eerily similar to my mother's death 20 years prior, in that they were both snatched away from my sister and I without warning. My father was a retired government employee, veteran, and most notably, Pastor of First Christ United Ministries in Baltimore, MD.

My parents were divorced when I was five. My mother raised my sister, Stacie, and I as a single mother for all but two years, and my dad got re-married. Twice. Growing up, we didn't see him much, even though we never lived more than five miles apart. What I do remember is his constant presence at my little league baseball games, him taking me to my first Orioles game at Memorial Stadium (and getting stung by a bee), him never missing a single high school football game of mine, and him always buying two gifts for our birthdays. The birthday kid got the bigger gift, but he always got a smaller gift for the other sibling. Eventually, when he was called to pastor and start his own church, my mom joined his church (You read that right. My mother joined her ex-husband's church where he was her pastor), which allowed us to see him every Sunday.

I was around 13 years-old and being able to see my father weekly as I navigated high school and into college was more precious than I even realized in the moment. That time made one thing clear to me: my father absolutely loved his children.

Those years helped to build a bond that, while not perfect and able to overcome everything, certainly helped us build a better relationship than statistics say we should have had. There were times growing up when I used to harbor negative feelings towards my father and wonder how he so easily raised his stepdaughter while we only got to see him on Sundays. I would question why she got to build relationships with my aunts, uncles, and cousins on his side of the family while my sister and I didn't. But even when those feelings crept into my heart, he was still my dad. He would still find ways to reassure us that we were loved and that we mattered most to him.

Fast forward to the year 2000. My mother passed away that August. That's when things changed for me. It was then, now as an adult myself; I could see certain things differently than I saw them as a kid. My father wasn't simply ignoring his kids. Right or wrong, he was trying to keep a happy home and made decisions he felt were best at that time. I decided I wasn't going to hold a grudge about the past and I would try to build the best relationship with my father I could going forward. Before you start rejoicing too much, this was real life, not a Disney special. This was much easier said than done.

What I began to realize in my father was that he was holding on to a lot of guilt and pain over how he physically neglected us as kids. I could see him beating himself up over past regrets and trying to "father" us now how he should have back then. My sister and I would always laugh when he'd attempt to parent us as 40-year-old adults when we both were parents of teenagers ourselves. The way he'd call us every birthday to sing "Happy Birthday" as if we were still 10. The text exchanges where we'd have to remind him that we're grown and know how to handle ourselves on social media. Then the voicemails with him exhorting, "This is your father. Call me back today!" that usually made us wait two more days to call him back. It was a constant back and forth of us trying to get him to appreciate the relationship we had and him trying to show us how much he loved us the best way he knew how.

It's amazing how hard it hits you when the birthday calls stop. When there are no more text messages and voicemails about which to complain. When all you want to do now is tell him how much you love and value him, when you hardly told him those things when he was alive and longed to hear them. When you look at pictures of yourself and you see you becoming him in every one of them. Thanks to COVID-19, I went all of 2020 without being able to see my father. The one time I saw him was that September day in his ICU bed to say, "Goodbye". As he lied there, sedated with only the ventilator keeping him alive, once he heard my sister and I speaking to him, he squeezed our hands and fought to get up. That was an intense moment that was unexpected and messed us both up!

All I remember saying to him was how thankful I am for the impact his presence had in my life. I realized in that moment, and in the months since his passing, that it doesn't always take physical presence to have an unforgettable impact on someone's life. My father's impact on me was far greater than I could begin to quantify. Space is no excuse for not being present in someone's life. Your time and your presence can be felt in many ways. My father made his impact on those Sundays. He made his impact at every event. He made his impact from his wheelchair and deathbed. His presence left an indelible mark on everything I am and will be. He was truly my greatest cheerleader in my adult life. If I was speaking, hosting an event, or releasing a book, he was either there in person, or the first one calling to tell me how proud he was of me. It's not too late for you to mend broken relationships and make your presence matter in the lives of those who mean the most to you. If not for yourself, do it for them. Make your time and presence matter.

MAKE YOUR LEADERSHIP MATTER

A genuine leader is not a searcher for consensus,
but a molder of consensus."
~ Rev Dr. Martin Luther King, Jr.

You do not need a title to be a leader. However, if you do have the title, do your best not to suck at it. Too often, people treat leadership like it's their favorite dessert. Everyone craves the dessert, but no one wants to eat their brussel sprouts first. There is a lot that goes into being a great leader. All of it isn't fun or even enjoyable. Sadly, having the title of leader doesn't automatically impart you with the wisdom to effectively lead. Being a leader is sexy. Who wouldn't want to experience the swag that comes with leadership? However, while the best leaders make it look easy, they all know just how difficult leadership can be.

I bet if you were to survey 100 people in leadership roles and asked if they considered themselves to be great leaders, 80-90% of them would reply in the affirmative. But the truth lies with those whom they lead. If you were to survey their direct reports and ask them if their leaders are great at leadership, I'd venture at least half of those leaders would be surprised by the responses they receive. We have all worked for horrible leaders, as well as seen horrible leaders at work. Over the past 4 years we witnessed exactly how dangerous inept, inexperienced, and immoral leadership can be to a country and a world. Poor leadership has an exponentially negative impact on those being led. Therefore, it is imperative you understand the impact your leadership has and to not take your role for granted.

I have written three books specifically on leadership, so I don't want to spend too much time on the matter. But for the sake of this book and creating impactful leadership, I want to share three quick points about the Top 3 Reasons Leaders Fail. I did an entire training on this in an episode of The Passionpreneur Podcast so I will share the abridged version.

Be sure to listen and subscribe the podcast, though. I could use the downloads.

Reason #1: Leaders fail because they are color blind.

In my position as the Director of Marketing and Development for a former nonprofit employer, during a meeting with an employee, we were reviewing a spreadsheet of potential donors. I was expressing to him what our game plan would be and how we would approach differing donors. As I was talking, I would give him directions like "Everyone highlighted in green will get a letter and every name in red needs to be removed from the list." The more I spoke, the more befuddled his countenance became. Eventually, I asked him what was confusing him. It was then that he informed me he was color blind. He couldn't discern all the colors on the spreadsheet! All the organizing and segmentation that made the data clearer for me, had subsequently made it far more ambiguous for him. After that, we figured out a better way to get the job done that fit his skillset better.

Fortunately for that guy, he had a great leader. Ha! But how many times do leaders make the mistake of assuming everyone on the team sees things the same way? Breakdowns from poor communication often stem from leaders assuming everyone "gets" what is being said, because it makes sense to the leader who said it. Never considering that subordinates who don't understand will more likely remain quiet about it rather than risk looking like they aren't qualified. The most impactful leaders take time to ask questions, listen to feedback, and adjust their own communication when necessary.

Reason #2: Leaders fail due to their inability to take decisive action.

When is the best time to buy a smoke detector? When everything is fine, or while the house is on fire? As a leader, you cannot wait until your organization is burning to then install smoke detectors. As I coach on impact leadership within organizations, one constant complaint I hear regarding organizational culture is teams who complain that their leader doesn't take decisive action when it comes to nipping potentially culture destroying employee behavior in the bud. We have all been there. We have all worked in environments where every single employee knows who the problem child is and they all but beg the leader to handle that person, yet the leader inexplicably ignores, or even worse, enables said behavior. I have watched an entire management team walk out the door because of how the Executive Director failed to admonish, and even rewarded poor performance from certain employees while fostering a culture of mistrust and backstabbing.

Your team expects you as their leader to take decisive action. If your team brings a problem to you, as their leader, they expect you to make the decisions and take the actions they cannot take. Failure to address negative culture breeds resentment amongst employees towards you as the leader. Your failure to act when necessary will cause you to lose your best people. You cannot allow one deadbeat to jeopardize your integrity as a leader and expect your team to ride for that. Stop ignoring the smoke detectors in your organization warning you of problems. Once you allow an inferno to rage, there is no rebuilding the destruction you accepted. No one is going to want to hear your suggestions and bright ideas on improving things after watching you allow the whole thing to burn while ignoring their alerts of danger.

Reason #3: Leaders fail because they lose the trust of their team.

Do you know what I have the most difficult time getting leaders to do? Let me spare you the guessing game. Leaders have the most difficult time admitting they made a mistake. I don't get it. Leadership does not equate to perfection. No one in their right mind expects their leaders to never make mistakes. I'd venture that if you aren't making mistakes as a leader, you aren't as impactful a leader as you may think. But you know what is even worse than making a mistake as a leader? Lying about it. No one trusts a liar. Your team will forgive your mistakes if they trust you. The minute you give them reason not to trust you, it's a wrap.

As I write this section, I am coming to realize one fact. I have really worked for some terrible bosses! But I digress. The point I want you to takeaway is, if you find yourself at the point as a leader where you are covering up more than you are sharing and spending more time making excuses than executing, just save everyone the added stress and leave. Once your team no longer trusts you to lead them, while they may not physically leave, they have already checked out mentally and planning their escape. You see it in sports when a team starts losing. The owners don't replace the stars, they replace the coach. They bring in a new voice to reach the players. It's the same game and same players, yet somehow the team starts winning. The change was the team's renewed trust in a leader and their willingness to go all out for a leader they trust.

MAKE YOUR FULFILLMENT MATTER

"D@mn right I like the life I live,
'cause I went from negative to positive."
~ The Notorious B.I.G.

I'm going to let you in on a little secret. Your happiness matters. You do not have to serve others at the peril of your own joy. Stated differently, helping others shouldn't hurt you. I don't know when and how we started believing that, because your purpose may be aligned with service to others, that your own joy and happiness must then be forfeited for the good of those whom you serve. It's one thing to make sacrifices in service to others, but never should those sacrifices repay you in pain. One sacrifice you should never be willing to make is your fulfillment.

Let's look at an example. You have an opportunity to do something you've always wanted to do. Whatever your thing is, imagine that. Doing this thing will help more people than you've been able to help before, so you're excited about the opportunity. But there are two caveats. The first caveat is: you won't be paid for the event. You know, it's one of those "sow into the ministry for good exposure" type deals. Secondly, it's the same day as your spouse's birthday. You're not married? OK, it's your child's birthday. No kids? Fine, your parent's. Ugh, your BFF's birthday! Just go with me for this illustration!

Here's the rub. Agreeing to do the event for free and missing the birthday is certainly a sacrifice that, depending on your situation, may be worth making. I've made that choice a time or two. Success absolutely requires sacrifice. But here's where sacrifice easily transforms into pain and may end up dealing you a hand you weren't expecting. Because you took this non-paying opportunity, you're still behind on your payments and your car is being repossessed. Better yet, you missed your spouse's birthday and unbeknownst to you, this was the last straw for them. Now when you return home, they're gone and left for good. Suddenly you are asking yourself if the sacrifice was worth it. It is difficult finding fulfillment when you're catching the bus and coming home to an empty house, waiting for that exposure to pay off. Please don't sell short the value of your fulfillment because someone else is trying to sell you a worthless sacrifice badge of honor. Your sacrifice should not come without fulfillment.

Fulfillment isn't only reserved for service and business. You deserve to find fulfillment in all areas of your life. I was having a conversation with one of our featured Make It Matter! Moment guests, Stanley Tate (you can watch that interview in the Make It Matter! online masterclass) about the danger of the word "should." How many times has someone suggested to you something you "should" do? "You paint so well; you should sell your artwork." "You are so funny on social media; you should start a podcast." Your cakes are so delicious; you should open a bakery." "You're 40 years old, you should be the boss by now." "You're still single? You should [fill in the blank with any number of things]." No matter their intent behind their suggestion, that small little word has caused so much pain to so many who look at their situations in life and compare them to the list of what their life "should" look like.

I'm not talking about evaluating goals here. I'm speaking to those lists we all keep in our minds about what success should look like, what love should look like, what our family should look like, what our finances and business should look like, and so on. Too often, we miss out on the positives of our situations and the fulfillment it may bring because we are too busy beating ourselves up over what those things should look like. Maybe you should simply bake those cakes and paint those pictures as a hobby because that's what actually enjoy and it fulfills you, instead of trying to turn everything into a hustle because someone else told you that you should.

3 EASY THINGS YOU CAN DO RIGHT NOW

As I close this chapter, it is important that I share with you a few easy things you can do right now to begin creating greater impact. It would be irresponsible of me to share all this great insight with you without then sharing some actionable steps you can take right away. Yep, I'm putting you to work on the very first chapter of this book.

1. Determine what matters to you and only do that.

The first step to creating great impact and living a life that matters is to determine what actually matters to you. Not what others have told you should matter. Not the things you do because you believe that's what you're supposed to do. But what really matters to you. What are those things that truly make you feel alive and fulfilled? Take an inventory of all the "stuff" you allow to fill your day. Make a list of all the people you allow to take up your time. Chart out all the ways you spend your time and money. Look at those things and start crossing off everything that doesn't create the impact you desire. Start pruning away all the things that distract you, keep you broke, waste your time, and leave you empty. Yes, even, uhh ESPECIALLY, the people. Get laser focused on what matters to you and commit to only pursuing those things. Do this and watch how quickly the stress sheds from your life and the joy returns.

2. Master your message and only speak that.

The Bible teaches us that the power of life and death are in the tongue. What are speaking into existence in your life? What negative talk are you consciously or subconsciously speaking that is sabotaging your impact and fulfillment? What great dreams of yours have you stopped speaking to daily because too many people told you your dreams were too crazy? What does your aura say when you walk into a room? It's time to take a renewed focus and ownership of the story your life is telling and how that impacts those around you. I want you to develop your very own Matter Statement. Companies have mission statements, but I want you to develop your own Matter Statement that will guide your thoughts and actions daily. Your Matter Statement will be your declaration of who you are, what you will and will not accept in your life, and what impact you deliver to the world. Speak that. Live that. Reject everything that is contrary to that.

3. Choose your audience and only speak to them.

One of the most liberating moments in my business (and life) came when I got comfortable saying "No" to prospective clients and people who wanted to be in my circle. I read a book long ago called Book Yourself Solid by Michael Port. The book teaches professional speakers how to book speaking engagements. One of the first lessons he teaches speakers is what he calls the "Red Velvet Rope Policy". You've seen red velvet ropes. What do they do? They block unauthorized people from entering restricted areas. It sounds crazy at first that anyone in business would reject business; however, all business isn't good business. You can't serve everyone and honestly you shouldn't want to. Acknowledge who your ideal audiences are in your professional, business, and personal life. People who respect what matters to you and align with your Matter Statement. Accept that those are your people and only speak to them. Stop giving unauthorized people access to restricted space in your mind. Put up your red velvet rope and trust that who God has for you, is for you and those are the only people you need.

If you're going to live life, you may as well make it matter.

I want to encourage you to make a commitment right now to creating a life that matters for yourself. Choose one area in your life and begin there. Once you improve that area, move on to another. If you will allow me, I want to coach you through this journey. In assembling this project, I brought together some of the brightest minds on how to create impact and fulfillment in your life. This book is only the beginning. This journey, just like yours, is ongoing. We have not only compiled this book, but we have taken the trainings even deeper in the form of an online masterclass. In the masterclass, you will find video trainings, interviews, and other resources from experts to help you fully immerse yourself in the journey of creating a life of impact and fulfillment.

While this book ends with these printed pages, the online masterclass is a living, breathing, ever-expanding resource. There will always be new video and audio trainings, live events, spotlight interviews, and resources added, so you don't want to miss out. If you haven't already secured your membership when you purchased the book, I encourage you to do so now by simply going to ***www.themakeitmatterproject.com/***

course or by pointing your cell phone's camera at the QR code below. As my gift to you, use the code MATTER for an extra discount.

Each author in this book is here to assist you and work with you. Don't just treat this book like just another self-help book. I'm thankful you purchased it, but I'll be even more excited to hear that you practiced it. If you know you still have more in you to give, and you desire a life that's more rewarding, then start creating that life today. I look forward to working with you more and helping you to MAKE IT MATTER!

* * *

To learn more by enrolling in Ryan's masterclass, point your cell phone's camera at the QR code then click the link:

LINDA
BUCKLEY

Linda is known as the Problem Solver. She doesn't focus on excuses; she focuses on solutions! She empowers people to believe in themselves and to think positive about their abilities and what they can accomplish in life.

With a degree from the University of Michigan Linda is a license clinical Social Worker. (LCSW) The Chicago native moved to Atlanta where she met her husband. She works in the health care field, and assisted patients and families with hospital medical trauma and mental health illness. She provided comprehensive assessments, consultation for emotional support, and community referrals.

She is an entertaining and dynamic speaker, Linda is a speaker, author and coach, who delivers useful information that will help you to improve your life and move forward. She speaks on topics such as dementia, women empowerment, and positive mental attitude. She counsels and couches adults to look at life in a positive manner.

Linda is a member of Toastmasters International and past President of Toastmasters of Centerville, where she helped the club to become President Distinguished many times. Linda has participated in many Speech contests and placed first in the International speech contest, first place in the Area Humorous speech contest. She has received the highest honor in Toastmasters Distinguished Toastmasters (DTM) three times. Toastmasters has helped her step into her greatness by building her confidence in speaking publicly to her community providing a needed service of empowerment.

Linda also has a passion for fitness and has ran many marathons. One in Nashville Tennessee; Bermuda, and Alaska. Her motto is," if you are going to train hard, go somewhere and enjoy the view."

CONTACT:

Website: www.ProblemSolvedBook.com

Email: Lbuckley1188@gmail.com

Facebook: Linda Buckley

LinkedIn: Linda Buckley

MAKE YOUR *Words* MATTER!

Did you know that you could destroy someone's self-image in a matter of a minutes? A parent can set the stage for a child's future behavior as a result of what they say in a manner that all that child's life they'll have to deal with what their parents said to them because the tongue can create great joy uplifting happiness peace a since of security, warmth, confidence and assurance or it can absolutely destroy all of that in a matter of moments.

Your words can be filled with magic and power.

A childhood rhyme "Sticks and stones may break my bones, but words can never hurt me." This is not true. Words can have a profound effect on how you behave and respond to others. Words have a strong impact on your life. Words can build you up or tear you down. Therefore, you should think before you speak because your words matter.

A study by Raymond Birdwhistle in 1970 proved that the words you speak to others represent just 7 percent of the results you get from your communication. The words you speak to yourself, however, generate 100 percent of the results you'll get in your life, as your own amazing mind interprets and follows your instructions.

When I was in the 5th grade, my teacher Mrs. Jones did an experiment. She had two healthy plants of the same species and height. She put them in the windowsill and gave them the same amount of food and water each day. The first plant was named Molly, the second plant was named Polly. We spoke to Molly in an incredibly positive manner. We said things like "You are pretty, you are growing tall, we love to watch you grow." We spoke to Polly in a very negative manner. We said, "You are ugly, you look stupid, you will never grow." We did this for the next 30 days. To our surprise, plant Molly grew 2 inches and was bright green. Plant Polly did not grow. She was drooping and turned yellow. We learned that words matter and that plants had feelings and emotions. The way we talk to plants can help them grow or not.

One was receiving bad energy and the other one was receiving positive energy. The impact of our words had a profound effect on the condition of the plants. She then related this to us and explained that how we talk to each other and ourselves really matters. Our classmates and other people can be affected by the words we say so we had to be careful not to use negative words toward our classmates. This experiment taught us to be kind to one another because words can affect us in a negative or positive manner. You may not realize how much words affect you.

After that experiment I really thought about how I spoke to others and the words that I was using. I used to say a lot of negative words to my classmates and myself, but after the experiment I changed the words that I had been saying. I no longer called people stupid or dumb. I no longer wished bad luck on anyone. My words became more positive and I became more helpful to others. I thought to myself if we can kill a plant because of the way we spoke to it, then how we were hurting each other when we say mean things.

You are where you are today because of what you have been saying to yourself. Your words are like seeds; when you speak, those words plant your future. The words you say become your reality. Whether you realize it or not, you may be calling forth your future. This is great when you are saying "I am worthy, I'm strong, and I will accomplish my goals." That's not just being positive—you are calling forth your success. Your life will move in the direction of your words. But too many people go around talking negative about their lives. They tell themselves "I am not worthy; I will never accomplish my dreams."

I can remember having a dismal outlook about going to college. I applied to many different colleges and thinking that I would never get accepted, because I was not college material, my grades were not good, and I was not smart. I worried that I would not have the money to pay for college. But I did not need money because my parents were going to pay for my college. If I did get into college, I thought that I would fail every class. I was thinking that I would have to leave college and come back home. This would be an embarrassment to my family.

I decided that I was not going to go to college. None of the classmates I associated with at school had plans for going to college. At lunch we talked about getting a job and not having to read another book. When we finished high school, learning would be over, and we would be free.

I remember in my English class. I had to give a speech. When the teacher called me to the front of the room, I thought I was ready. But when I got in front of the class, I stumbled over my words and forgot what I wanted to say. I just stood there staring at my classmates, then I ran to my seat. I felt like I was the dumbest person in the room. I knew that I would get an F for that speech. If I did get an F, to me it was a sign to drop out of school. I was feeling stressed and anxious.

After I sat down, I said a lot of negative words to myself. How could I be so dumb? Why didn't I remember what I wanted to say? Then I thought everyone in the class thought I was dumb.

During high school, I thought I had to be perfect. I thought that every test that I had failed or did not complete, the college would find out and that would give them a reason to deny me admission. Well, I really did not have to worry about that because I had made up my mind that I was not going to college. I was thinking it was a waste of time, I would be better off getting a job and making money.

My parents sat me down and wanted to know why I was so negative about going to college. I told them that I did not think I could do the work. I was not smart, and I forgot my speech in front of the class. After my parents listened to what I had to say, they told me that I would need to change the way I was thinking. I was too negative. I told them that I did not know how to change my thinking.

They gave me positive things to read, Motivational CD's to listen too, and affirmation to read daily. These things began to work, and my thinking started to change. I did become more positive. I had a different outlook on life and my abilities. I went to college and I did very well.

People do not realize how they are calling forth defeat, mediocrity, and lack by the negative words they are saying. When you put negative words in your life, you get negative results. You need to plant positive thoughts, just like you plant positive seeds. When you plant apples, you get apples. When you plant oranges, you get oranges. When you plant pears, you get pears. You are putting your words into action. You are planting the right kind of seeds. You need to plant the right kind of words. You can't plant poison ivy seeds and expect a positive outcome. You can't talk negative and expect to live a positive life. You can't talk defeat and expect to have joy. You can't talk lack and expect to have abundance. If you have a negative mouth, you're going to have a negative life. If you don't like what you are seeing, change it by saying positive words. Instead of saying: "I'll never get well. I always feel sick."

Start saying "I am getting well. I feel healthy. I'm getting better and better every day." You keep planting those words and seeds and eventually your words and life will be healthy. Start talking increase, abundance, and prosperity. "Blessing are coming my way. The right people and opportunities are coming my way." If you keep talking like this, good things will come your way. We have the power in ourselves to change our lives by the words we say to ourselves. We can bless our lives or we can curse our lives. Many people don't realize they are cursing their future with their negative words. Sometimes others don't have to defeat us; we defeat ourselves. Pay attention to what you are saying to yourself. Your words can trap you and can cause you to stumble. They can keep you from your potential. You're trapped by what you think. The same way I was trapped about going to college. Negative thoughts come to all of us. When you say them out loud, you give them life. That's when they become real. Don't set limits in your mind. You can change the way you talk to yourself and get out of the trap. Start speaking joy and positivity into your life. Be bold saying those things you're dreaming about, those things you're believing. When faced with adversity speak words of joy. Negative words can keep you from becoming who you were created to be.

You can pray in faith ask God to turn it around to do the impossible, but then walk away and start talking about how you're not going to get well, or how your child is never going to straighten up. Those negative words just cancelled out that prayer, I am having a financial crisis and I prayed and asked god to help me but, I don't see how it's going to happen, you've done it for me in the past I know you'll do it for me again in the future. Don't let your words trap you in negative thinking. That's what allows God to do the impossible. When you are faced with adversity, you must change your thinking and speak joy over your situation. You may feel fear but speak joy. There are always two voices fighting for your attention: the voice of Negativity and the voice of Positivity. You get to choose which voice comes to life. The voice of Negativity may seem louder, but you can take away all its power by choosing the voice of Positivity.

You can speak your goals and write them down. You should write down what you want to see happen in your life in any areas that you are struggling or need to improve. Write it down like it's already done. Then every day say that goal. Read it out loud several times a day. It's not enough to just think it, something happens when we speak it. You must speak your future. You can personalize yours goals, I am strong, I am healthy, I am in shape, I weigh what I'm supposed to weigh! I am full of energy, I am passionate, I am talented, I am secure, I am valuable, I am confident, I have a good personality, people like me. I am fun to be around! I am happy, I enjoy life, I am a person of excellence. I am full of integrity, I am successful, I'm am prosperous, my future is bright. My legacy will live on to inspire future generations. If you keep speaking positively over your life, those words will plant themselves inside of you. They'll not only change your outlook, but they will change who you are. Your words will become your reality.

I want you to listen to yourself for one full day listen to what you are saying to yourself and realize how your thoughts and emotions create situations in your life. Your words become your reality.

This is how you change the way you speak to yourself.

- Program yourself with positive thoughts by listening to positive and motivational messages every day for at least one hour. Listen to messages that get you moving, make you smile and think. These messages get in your mind and you will find yourself thinking about these messages every day. You will start to think and speak positive words rather than negative words. Have you ever thought about what you wanted but it appeared to be impossible, so you talked yourself out of it? This is where those positive messages you have been listening to and reading become real to you. They override the negative messages to help you reach the impossible. Your environment and people you associate with become positive.
- Be aware of who you are. It will help you to become a better leader, which will help you to succeed and talk to yourself in a positive and loving manner. Your success begins with you.
- Invest time in yourself . Close your eyes and look at your life. Are things the way you'd like them to be? If not, write down the way you want your life to be don't give one speck of mental energy to how it's going to happen. Just focus on what you want. Next, think about why you want the things you want. Finally, think about the how you will accomplish what you want. These steps are going to help you start the process.

If you are a negative person or want to change your thoughts about yourself, you can do this by using positive affirmations. Affirmations are sentences aimed to affect the conscious and the subconscious mind so in turn, they affect your behavior, thinking patterns, habits, and environment. The following is how you can use affirmations to affect your daily life

1. When using affirmations, you will need to be consistent and repeat them twice per day.
2. Start in the morning as soon as you wake up. This ensures you have a positive start to the day.
3. Say your second set before going to bed. This ensures that you have positive thoughts in your mind as you sleep.
4. Say your affirmations multiple times with a slow, confident voice.
5. Make a commitment to do them for 30 days. Don't give up.

Examples of affirmations:

- I am confident.
- I am my own superhero.
- I am adventurous
- I am love.

I have used affirmations and positive self-talk most of my life. I have seen a difference in my life and the way I responds to others. The difference is that I am more positive and upbeat about life. I have a set of affirmations that I say in the morning and in the evening just before bed. I usually read motivational stories and inspirational messages so that I can think and reflect on the goodness of life. This helps me to stay focus on what is good about life rather than what is negative. There are so many negative things on TV that you need something positive to cancel out the negative.

I think about what I am going to say before I say it because you can't take the words you say back. I also try not to talk negative about other people, even if I know their faults. I try not to lie or state idle gossip. I appreciate when others tell me that I am talking negative about someone.

What I would like for you to do after reading my chapter is to set up a discovery call to see how I can move you from negative to positive thinking. I want to help you to overcome your negative thinking and to have a positive outlook on life. There are so many ways we can help to make your life better. Stop thinking defeat and think victory. You have the power to change. Your words matter!

* * *

To learn more by enrolling in Linda's masterclass, point your cell phone's camera at the QR code then click the link:

GREGORY L.
CARTER

Gregory L. Carter's passion for helping clients and empowering them to make more informed decisions that lead to peace in their retirement years, has led him to serve as Managing Partner of Carter Financial. He leads a team of professionals with 50 years of combined experience in financial planning, college funding, career development coaching, business consulting, and corporate funding. The team consist of Fiduciaries, Retirement Planners, Tax Strategist, Healthcare Experts, Estate Planners, and Business Consultants.

Greg holds a Bachelor of Science degree in Management from Hampton University and a Master of Science degree in Administration from Central Michigan University. He is an Accredited Small Business Consultant® and a Certified Financial Fiduciary®. Greg is a past president of the Atlanta Chapter of the American Financial Education Alliance (AFEA) and is a member of the Association of Accredited Small Business Consultants®, the National Association of Certified Financial Fiduciaries® and the National Association of Insurance and Financial Advisors. In his spare time, Mr. Carter enjoys golfing, traveling, volunteering at church and spending time with his three children who are in college, high school and middle school.

CONTACT:

Gregory L. Carter, ASBC® CFF

Office: 404 713-5022

Online: *carterfinancial.us*

Email: *info@carterfinancial.us*

Instagram: *@carter_financial*

Facebook: *@CarterFinancialATL*

MAKE YOUR *Money* MATTER!

Two-time Academy Award-winning actor Denzel Washington was asked about the importance of money and he answered by saying, "Money doesn't buy happiness. Some people say it is a heck of a down payment, though." Financial expert Dave Ramsey says, "Earning a lot of money is not the key to prosperity. How you handle it is." The Holy Bible says this about money, "But you shall remember [with profound respect] the Lord your God, for it is He who is giving you power to make wealth, that He may confirm His covenant which He swore (solemnly promised) to your fathers, as it is this day." Deuteronomy 8:18 (AMP)

Money means different things to different people. It can represent safety, security, freedom, and so on. I have found that to earn, save, and grow money, you must treat it seriously and not casually. After all, anything you treat casually in life will become a casualty: Your faith, your relationships, your education, your career, and certainly your money. This is true for the hundreds of clients I have served, and it is true for my own experience with money.

In early 2009, I learned a painful lesson about the danger in treating money casually. My story begins in April of 2008 when I was downsized from the Fortune 500 corporation where I spent 15 years climbing the ladder from college intern to mid-level executive. I will refer to this corporation as Company A.

Though my executive position was eliminated, I left with a severance package equal to one year of salary, fully vested stock options, a lump sum pension balance, and a sizeable 401k balance. In fact, I had even secured my next corporate position ahead of my last day on payroll at Company A. I was winning! So how could I go wrong with all those things going for me?

Before I explain my painful financial lesson from 2009, here is a bit of additional background. My mentor at Company A was a successful, senior-level-corporate executive, who retired after an illustrious 30-year career. I will call him Henry. Naturally, Henry was and still is my role model and mentor.

As a young man, I saved a good amount of money for retirement based on the example of Henry and his wife. They have worked with the same financial advisor for the past 35 years. Despite Henry's example and coaching, I must admit that I really did not understand how to make my money matter for my future. I will expand on that shortly.

Back to the spring of 2008 when I was poised to leave Company A–the only company I had ever worked for. Because I had solid retirement assets and savings for my age, Henry recommended that I work with his financial advisor to develop a financial plan. This was scary for me to trust someone with my life savings.

Henry's financial advisor was too busy to take me on as a client himself. So, he introduced me to a very capable, younger, advisor in his firm. I will call her Carol. She was genuinely nice and listened to the goals that my spouse and I had at the time.

Next came Carol's plan on how to invest the retirement assets I had acquired over 15 years. We were pleased with the plan Carol presented and moved forward with her recommendations.

Even if you are not a student of economics, you will recall what happened to the financial markets in September 2008. There was a severe worldwide economic crisis considered by many economists to have been the most serious financial crisis since the Great Depression of the 1930s. This financial crisis happened months after I engaged Carol to manage my retirement assets. Because Carol did not protect my retirement assets properly, I experienced severe financial pain when the stock market crashed in September 2008. By early 2009 I had lost 1/3 of my retirement savings to negative stock market performance!

Carol failed to use the growth and protection strategy that I now use for my clients. In fact, this experience in 2009 with Carol is what led me to leave my corporate position and become a financial advisor a few years later. I vowed to educate and protect client's money using the financial strategies that I will outline for you in this chapter. My mission is to MAKE MY CLIENT'S MONEY MATTER now and in the future.

The loss I suffered in 2008 was the largest financial failure of my life. However, I believe that failure can be the path to success. If and only if you are humble and learn from the pain to course correct. I often say to my clients, "The future depends on what you do today…" Today, I will cover seven financial strategies to MAKE YOUR MONEY MATTER to achieve financial success.

Strategy #1 – Income Planning

I really enjoy working with clients who say, "Greg, we want to retire on our terms without worrying about money." This desire challenges me to ensure that the client's expenses can be paid month to month with reliability and predictability for the rest of their lives. This includes a review of social security benefits, income and expense analysis, inflation planning, spousal planning, and longevity protection. The goal is for the client to walk to the "mailbox" each month in retirement and collect a check that covers their expenses.

To implement an income plan that meets your needs in retirement, hire a financial advisor who operates with your best interest as his or her guide. There is a lot of misinformation and misunderstanding about how retirement savings must be converted into retirement income. A highly competent financial advisor will help you establish an income plan that withstands the test of time, regardless of what happens in the financial markets. You should also work with a financial advisor who utilizes a strategy that is guaranteed to grow and protect your money against investment losses, economic downturns, and excessive management fees.

Warren Buffet, the man many consider to be the most successful investor of all time, has two rules of investment success. Rule #1 is Never Lose Money. Rule #2 is Never Forget Rule #1. I often imagine where my retirement savings would be today if Carol utilized the growth and protection strategy for me in 2008 that I implement for my clients today. I certainly would not have lost 1/3 of my retirement savings during the 2008 stock market crash.

To ensure that your income plan is designed and built properly, you should discuss the following questions with your financial advisor:

- Is my retirement money safe?
- Is it guaranteed?
- If not, can I afford to lose some of it?

If your money is invested in stocks, bonds, and mutual bonds, you should know that ten years of market gains can be completely wiped out in only ten weeks of market losses as they were in 2008 when I had my most painful financial lesson. When I work with clients to develop an income plan, I recommend solutions that protect and grow their savings with a guarantee of no market losses.

Strategy #2 – Investment Planning

Once I have worked with a client to establish an income plan, I create an investment plan for the remaining assets that are not needed to draw from month to month in retirement. This typically includes a risk tolerance assessment, portfolio fee analysis, volatility control, and comprehensive Institutional Money Management.

As you work with a financial advisor to establish an investment plan, I highly recommend that you discuss these questions upfront.

- How much income is needed for retirement?
- How long do you need your money to last in retirement?
- How safe is your retirement money?
- What cost is associated with any investment you consider?

When I work with clients, my goal is to grow any additional retirement assets that are not needed for the income plan by utilizing investments that are safe, with low fees and good annual returns. These investments often yield significant tax advantages as well.

Strategy #3 – Tax Planning

The most significant difference between the wealthy and the middle class is the time the wealthy spend thinking of ways to minimize their taxes. But nobody likes paying taxes. Taxes can eat away at your retirement savings growth, potentially decimating your ability to save for retirement.

Any comprehensive retirement plan will include a strategy for decreasing tax liabilities. This typically includes assessing the taxable nature of your current holdings, tax-free planning, tax category income timing analysis, and inheritance planning.

When Henry retired after 30 years from Company A, he left with an excellent retirement package. He had 401k savings, a pension for life, deferred compensation, healthcare, and many other benefits. Henry's favorite retirement benefit is his deferred compensation program. He continues to enjoy income from this program 20 years after retirement.

Companies offer deferred compensation plans as an incentive to executives. The plans include tax advantages for deferring a percentage of the executive's salary for a set number of years. The deferred portion of the salary plus interest is returned to the executive after the defined period of years.

I work with my clients to create these deferred income plans regardless of their job title. The following is an example of a deferred compensation plan I implemented for a client who needed a 'bucket' of tax-free savings in retirement:

- Client aged 37 deferred $10,000 annually for 12 years.
    - At age 60, an annual tax-free income stream of $25,000 begins and continues until age 90.
    - Plan includes $400,000 in life insurance coverage during the client's working years.
    - Plan includes living benefits that provide over $250,000 in the event of a serious, critical, chronic, or terminal illness.

The deferred compensation plan outlined above offers the following benefits for retirement savers:

- Contributions guaranteed
- No investment losses ever
- All investment gains locked in with annual reset
- Tax-free income

- Penalty-free access to account value at any time
- Life insurance coverage included
- Living benefits included

Finally, there are investments that provide significant tax advantages. Once again, you must work with a financial advisor who has your best interest in mind and who has access to solutions that meet your needs.

The following is an example of an alternative investment that yields a double-digit return and a dollar-for-dollar tax offset in the tax year that the investment is made:

- Client received $100,000 in additional income in a tax year from a severance package payment equal to 1 year of salary. Client needed to offset taxes on the additional income. The following solution was utilized:
    - Client makes a one-time investment of $100,000 from a 401k held at a previous employer
    - Investment is in a tax-advantaged alternative investment with a 3 to 5 term
    - Fixed dividend of 12% paid to client annually
    - Client receives a $100,000 tax-deferral for the year of the investment
    - Investment is free from stock-market volatility
    - Principal investment is returned to client at the end of the term

As I mentioned, I left Company A in 2008 with a significant retirement savings in 401k, pension, and severance. However, all three of those savings sources were taxable. Carol DID NOT recommend any tax-advantaged investment options for me to build a "tax-free bucket" of income in the future. Today when I work with clients, I invest their money in a way that will minimize the effect of taxes on their savings potential.

Strategy #4 – Healthcare Planning

Even though Henry has worked with the same financial advisor for 35 years with great success, there is a glaring omission in his financial plan. His financial advisor did not establish a plan to cover the cost of healthcare over and above Medicaid or Henry's retiree health insurance. That means that Henry and his wife will be forced to utilize their retirement assets to cover the cost of long-term care should they need it. The cost could be for skilled nursing in the home, assisted living or treatment for a chronic illness. It was not until I became a financial advisor that Henry realized this glaring omission in his financial plan.

According to the US Department of Health and Human Services two out of three of us will eventually require some sort of assisted living, home nursing, convalescent, hospice, or custodial care. These are often referred to as elder care services. But these elder care services are not covered by Medicare or by Medicare supplements. The cost of elder care services can range from $3,000 to $7,000 per month, depending on where one lives, and the level of care or assistance required. A person may require this care for a few months or for several years.

If you do not have a healthcare plan to cover elder care services, you will have to use money from your savings, or your family will have to pay the expenses for you or take you into their homes. This can be a financial and lifestyle imposition on your family with a loss of privacy and independence for you. I have seen this scenario firsthand with members of my family and with clients who are caring for elderly parents.

I work with my clients to create a plan to address rising healthcare costs with a minimum of expense. According to the Employee Benefits Research Institute, a 65-year-old couple with median prescription-drug expenses who retire this year will need $295,000 to enjoy a 75 percent chance of being able to pay all their remaining lifetime medical bills, and $360,000 to have a 90 percent chance. Those figures will only grow over the years as the cost of healthcare rises.

Strategy #5 – Estate Planning

I would argue that no strategy for the future is complete without an estate plan. Sadly, 70% of Americans have NO estate plan. Yet every day, 137 people die in auto accidents, and 14,000 others die from a heart attack, cancer, or other causes.

Consider that for a moment. More than 14,000 people of all ages die every day. Each one of these people leave their families with all their financial obligations, all their legal liabilities, and the responsibilities for numerous decisions. These are decisions that can result in unnecessary expenses, taxes, and debts. These choices may also impact the lives of their dependents and alter family dynamics for generations.

Here are a few examples of these decisions:

- Guardian(s) for minor children if both parents die in a car accident
- Care for a disabled or special needs adult when elderly parents pass on
- Financial and healthcare decisions for someone in a coma or someone who is mentally incapable of making decisions
- Settle debts or taxes for a deceased person
- Transfer property rights
- Sharing rules for a deceased person's assets or income

Decisions like these quite often result in contentious arguments and dissension and even animosity among heirs, creditors, and business partners. This could tie up income and assets in probate court for years. I cannot think of a more devasting issue for a grieving family to contend with as they struggle to heal. Because of this, I work collaboratively with a qualified Estate Planning Attorney to help my clients establish a comprehensive estate plan.

Strategy #6 – Risk Management Planning

An executive at a top insurance carrier once said, life insurance is like a parachute; if you do not have it the first time you need it, there is no second chance. When you think about that analogy, surely you must ask yourself "Do I have my parachute, packed, tested and ready in the event of a serious, critical, chronic illness or worse?"

Most people purchase life insurance to provide a legacy of financial security at the time of their death. But they do not always consider benefits that can extend and be available for the difficult financial times they must face if a chronic, critical, or terminal illness precedes death. The life insurance industry calls the benefit an "Accelerated Death Benefit Rider." As referenced earlier in the deferred compensation example, these benefits are also referred to as living benefits.

After all, most parents make an unspoken promise to themselves to protect and provide for their family now and in the future – no matter what! To illustrate why life insurance with living benefits is so important, I offer the following diagram:

Living Benefits

Life Insurance with Living Benefits

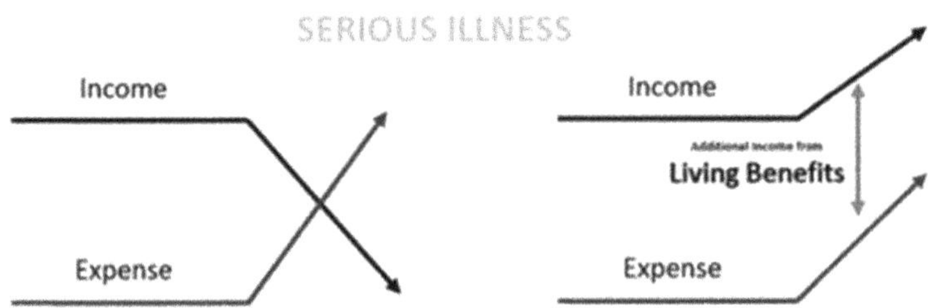

Protecting your highest priority with proper life insurance planning keeps your promise intact

This diagram tells us the following:

- When a serious illness or worse happens in a family, income goes down because someone is no longer working, and expenses typically increase because of medical bills.
- If a life insurance policy with living benefits is in place prior to an illness or death, the income line is adjusted to match the increase in expenses.
- Living benefits allow the insured person to accelerate up to 90% of their life insurance death benefit for income when diagnosed with a serious, critical, chronic, or terminal illness.

The importance of life insurance with living benefits coverage became crystal clear for me when I received a referral to help another family a few years ago. The new clients had endured a devasting illness the year before I met them.

The illness was a brain aneurysm that struck the husband and father of two small children while at work. I will call this gentleman Mr. J. He was in his early 40's and a successful corporate executive. Mr. J had a mild stroke caused by the brain aneurysm. By the grace of God, he made a recovery after several months. However, his life would never be the same.

Mr. J could no longer hold his corporate position after his recovery. It was a struggle for him to remember things, and his speech was impaired. Fortunately, his company had a good healthcare plan that paid him 40% of his salary for one year. This loss of his income caused his wife to take on a second job to keep the house afloat financially.

When I met Mr. J and his wife, they shared their financial goals with me, and I reviewed their existing financials. I discovered that Mr. J and his wife did not have a life insurance policy with living benefits. Mr. J did have $500,000 in life insurance coverage with a reputable insurance carrier, but it did not include a living benefits provision. If he had a policy with living benefits prior to his brain aneurysm, the home mortgage and other debt could have been paid off to reduce household expenses.

This story literally broke my heart. Even if you do not heed my previous advice, please work with a financial advisor to put life insurance with living benefits in place for yourself and others who depend on you.

Strategy #7 – College Planning

In 2015, the average four-year cost for a public university was $84,000, and a private college was $190,000 per child. In 2020, a family can easily exceed $250,000 in college costs for one child. Most families do not realize that there are two different prices for a college education. A price for the informed buyer and a price for the uninformed buyer. Which price do you think most families would prefer to pay?

I offer a specialized college-planning capability that helps families become informed buyers of a college education, helping to reduce their out-of-pocket college costs. With this service, a family can answer these vitally important questions:

- Will we have to pay the school's sticker price?
- Which schools would attract my child with financial inducements?
- Which schools offer tuition discounts based on my student's academic performance?
- Can we increase our financial aid eligibility?
- Will we qualify for tax credits? Which ones?
- Would test prep benefit our child?

A high percentage of the clients I work with for financial planning have significant student loan debt that holds them back from optimal retirement saving. I highly recommend that you work with a college planning expert to explore the most cost-effective way for your family to provide a college education for your children.

We have certainly covered a lot of information. My hope is that this information will allow you to **MAKE YOUR MONEY MATTER.**

If you are ready to design and build your solid financial house, I am prepared to roll up my sleeves and assist you. In fact, it is my calling to help families and individuals protect and grow their money to enjoy the future that they want and deserve.

Over the next 30 days, I challenge you to make a list of the seven strategies that I have covered and rate yourself. Simply give yourself a plus (+) or minus (-) on where you stand against each strategy.

If you have more minuses than pluses or want to have all pluses, reach out to my firm so that we can help you. You can reach us at the following destinations online or by phone:

carterfinancial.us / (404) 713-5022 / info@carterfinancial.us

Simply schedule a no-obligation, complimentary, phone consultation with us to discuss your needs and goals. My team and I will provide a view of where you are versus where you want to be. The next step is totally up to you.

Can you imagine how differently you will feel knowing that your financial future has been designed and built for high success? I can imagine how you would feel because I have personally heard from a multitude of clients who thank my team and me for guiding them. I want that for you as well.

Contact us today because the future depends on what you do today. I cannot wait to meet you and work with you to **MAKE YOUR MONEY MATTER!**

Note that my firm, Carter Financial, is an independent financial services firm helping individuals create retirement strategies using a variety of investment and insurance products to custom suit their needs and objectives. Investing involves risk, including the potential loss of principal. No investment strategy can guarantee a profit or protect against loss in periods of declining values. Any comments regarding safety and guaranteed income streams refer only to fixed insurance products. They do not refer, in any way to securities or investment advisory products. Insurance and Annuity product guarantees are subject to the claims-paying ability of the issuing company. No legal advice, options or recommendations are being made in respect to this proposal. You should consult your tax professional or attorney concerning such advice and opinions.

* * *

To learn more by enrolling in Gregory's masterclass, point your cell phone's camera at the QR code then click the link:

DR. ASHLEY
DASH

Dr. Ashley Dash inspires action through her lived experiences in person and online. She often shares her greatest life challenges, including how she went from being an unemployed college graduate to landing a $100k+ job in Human Resources with Mercedes-Benz. Or revealing how years later, she restarted her life after facing foreclosure and unemployment, shifting back to six-figures with an international move to Japan.

Dr. Dash is known for her ability to help individuals identify the patterns that keep them stuck and move them into action. She is determined to create safe spaces for black business professionals in Corporate America through speaking, coaching, and courses using her high energy and direct approach. Her mission is to help people overcome personal circumstances, regain control of their lives, and find purpose through career freedom. A self-proclaimed information junkie, she believes in Faith over Facts and Facts over Feelings.

Dr. Ashley Dash has a Bachelor of Science in Business Administration, an MBA, and a Doctorate of Strategic Leadership. She is also a Certified Job and Career and Development Coach and Job and Career and Transition Coach. However, celebrating and loving Black men remains her best and all-time favorite superpower.

CONTACT:

www.DrAshleyDash.com

To book a Career Freedom Strategy Session:

www. workwithdrashleydash.com

Facebook: http://facebook.com/drashleydash

LinkedIn: https://www.linkedin.com/in/ashleygaryroper/

MAKE YOUR *Legacy* MATTER!

Discovering the Key to Generational Wealth and Creating a Life Beyond Your Wildest Dreams

On my first day back in the office after the Christmas holiday in 2019, I was fired from my first and only nonprofit job. While the organization was fantastic and had a great mission, my heart was not in it. Partly because I was not getting paid the six-figure salary I was accustomed to, and partly because I did not want to be there. It was a great position, just not the right role for me. I was somewhat relieved when my hiring manager called me into her office first thing in the morning to let me go. It meant I did not have to continue showing up pretending this job is where I wanted to be. When in fact, I would rather work on my consulting business and felt this job was getting in my way. Although I was caught off guard at the moment, looking back in hindsight, I was not surprised. However, I found myself struggling with my coaching practice, as well. Honestly, the business was slow, and I could not seem to catch a break or get focused on landing clients to reach profitability. Sales were slim to none, and it just seemed like the harder I worked, the easier it was for everything to fall apart. As my business failed, my career ended right before my eyes; I could hear my grandmother's voice in my ear saying, "You've got a good job Ashley, you better hold on to it." I wanted to heed her well-meaning advice; however, I could not shake the feeling that there was more to life than a good job and a decent salary. What about my purpose? What about doing something I loved and got paid well to do? Were unemployment and failed entrepreneurial plans going to be my legacy?

I am sharing this with you is because you need to know that you DESERVE more. You deserve a life filled with purpose and financial stability. You deserve career freedom and a legacy that matters. Today people know me as Dr. Dash, Career Branding Expert™, founder of National Black Man Day™, and Global HR Consultant living the dream in Japan. However, before all the fancy titles and accolades, I was Ashley the Recession Baby, an unemployed college graduate whom no one would touch with a ten-foot pole right before the Great Recession in 2008.

No one can predict what happens in life. Life will always change and throw unexpected curveballs. In 2018 life changed for me in the most unexpected ways. I moved to Atlanta, Georgia, for a fresh start, a chance to be closer to family and watch my nephews grow up. I never thought I would be an aunt, so hearing my nephews scream "TT" excitedly whenever they saw me was a blessing I did not know existed. However, the excitement dimmed far too quickly as I faced eviction and began couch-surfing with family and friends. As a 32-year-old adult with a master's degree, I can say this is not where I saw my life; single, unemployed, and broke. I felt like my life was on this vicious repeating pattern I could not seem to escape.

I was initially excited about landing a great job, only to see the excitement fizzle within six months or less while longing for something more. Regardless of how much money I was making, from $50,000 - $100,000+, there did not seem to be any job that could hold my interest or keep me motivated. Looking back, what I failed to understand clearly, was that I was the contributing factor in all of these situations. My decisions. My actions. My story. What I have learned is the key to building a widely successful legacy and living a life one is excited about is YOU. You are the key. Despite what the world tells you and what you tell yourself, you are WORTHY. What you have is all you need. You ARE enough. You already have everything you need to succeed. You have to shift your mindset and believe. You have to MAKE YOUR LEGACY MATTER. You may not believe me right now, but you do not need another degree, certification, relationship, or marriage to validate the legacy you are building.

Yes, I said "building" as in present tense. Your legacy is not off in some distant future where you leave millions of dollars of inheritance to your family, friends, and charities of your choice, although that is pretty awesome. You are creating your living legacy right now. Your legacy shows up every day in every way with your decisions, whether you see it or not. All you need is the person you see in the mirror each day.

I have learned and shared with my clients that legacy planning is an active daily process. People push legacy planning and building into the future, a future that never comes. Far too many individuals consider the future a distant point wherein their minds, they have finally "arrived." But honestly, this could not be further from the truth. Life will always change, and often what we imagine our lives to be, do not show up the way we dreamed or even perhaps prayed for. When this happens, we delay our legacy. We push it off further because the time is not right.

But newsflash: There will never be a time like the present to begin building your legacy. Whether you are broke, broken, or fired like me in the past, all you have is all you need to start your legacy. You CAN create a life beyond your wildest dreams and begin fulfilling your legacy TODAY. Whether you believe what has been shared thus far or not, trust if you are reading these words, you are EXACTLY where you need to be to begin building generational wealth, and the first step is career freedom.

So, you may be asking yourself, what exactly is career freedom? First, we will begin with what career freedom is not. Career freedom is not just about fancy cars, high fashion labels, multiple homes, and seven-figure investment accounts. Although career freedom can include these items, this only scratches the surface of what it is. True career freedom is about having a choice. It is a choice to wake up early to go to a job you hate or waking up early excited to see the sunrise. You choosing to take a mental health day from your stressful job or creating memories with family and friends on a dream vacation. The option to live the life you see in your head or merely settling and accepting the life you have right now.

Career freedom is about creating a life where you are in control, you make the decisions, and you create effortless job security for life. Not security, which comes from staying at a job you hate because the money is good, but the KNOWLEDGE of whether the country is in a recession or not, you are going to be okay. Regardless if the president is a Democrat or Republican, life is going to be great. Meaning, even if you get fired right now today, it does not and will not matter. You have everything you need inside you to succeed; you need a plan to make it happen.

It is important to remember that career freedom is only the first step on the three-way path to creating generational wealth and creating a living legacy. Creating a common language and understanding is crucial for everyone's success. Therefore, we will look at all three steps needed to make a living legacy using the illustration below before diving deeper into career freedom.

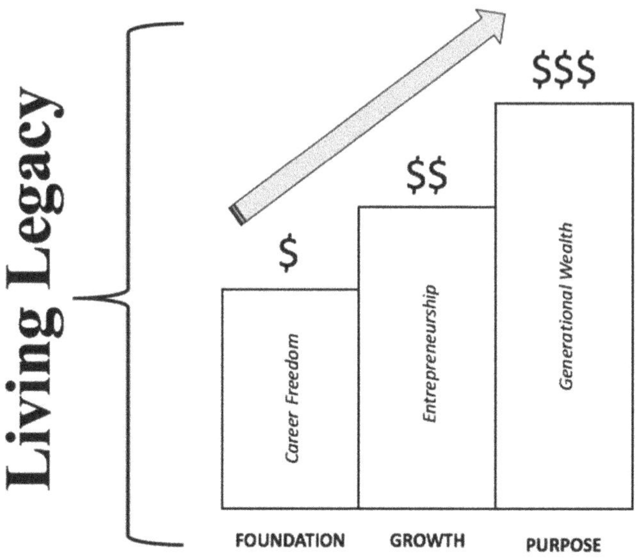

The first step in creating a Living Legacy is the Foundation: Career Freedom, which means taking control of your career, so you have a choice. Whether you are in Corporate America or a full-time entrepreneur, true career freedom is less about what you do and more about you having a choice in how you work, where you live, and how much money you make. The goal here is not only financial, but about learning to leverage time and resources, so you have the space to create the life you want. Many people try to skip this step and head straight to purpose, but it is the most important.

The next step is Growth: Entrepreneurship. Whether you know it or not, you are already an entrepreneur. Entrepreneurship is not all about starting businesses and creating LLCs. According to the Merriam-Webster Dictionary, an entrepreneur is someone who manages risk. Even if you are a corporate employee, you are already in the entrepreneurship game if you have a 401k or IRA. Investments are all about risk and risk tolerance. This stage's goal is growing money without growing the amount of time it takes to make or manage it. However, it is essential to ensure a strong foundation of financial stability before moving forward.

The last step, the one most people are most interested in, is Purpose: Generational Wealth. This point is where you can create a lasting impact. Generally, people are excited about the idea of getting paid to do what they love. At this step, people get PAID MORE to DO LESS. Think of all the successful people operating in their purpose, Oprah Winfrey, Jay-Z, Beyonce, Barack and Michelle Obama, or Michael Jordan. They have career freedom, can grow money through entrepreneurial activities without the exclusive use of their time, and create generational wealth using their purpose.

Rarely do people skip straight to working on their purpose. For many, the journey to creating career freedom is a winding road. It is often difficult to know the support you need and when you need it, so I created a framework for finding career freedom. This diagram can pinpoint precisely where you are, where you want to be, and the gap you need to overcome to ensure success. Not only are there multiple levels to career freedom, but strategies for each stage to help you create a life beyond your wildest dreams.

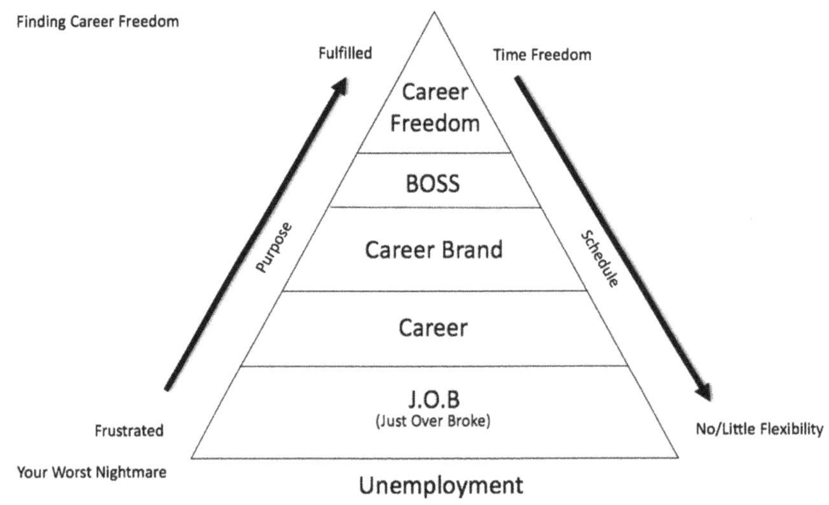

The first level is unemployment. As an independent adult with bills and responsibilities, this is everyone's worst nightmare. Typically, unemployment means no job, no business, and no income. However, I would argue that even if you are making some money, you still fall into this category if it is not enough to survive. Generally, people who fall in this category make less than $12,000 a year. When someone is unemployed, the goal is not to jump to the top of the pyramid but to reach income stability and security by landing a stable job. The strategy here is taking action with an effective job search strategy. People should not be afraid to ask for help through referrals, find job leads, and take action by submitting multiple applications. This way, they can stop stressing financially about essentials such as food, clothing, and shelter.

The second level in the framework is a J.O.B., also known as just over broke. Unfortunately, many people, myself included, take this particular level for granted because we do not feel fulfilled and are itching for something more. At this level, there is not much flexibility, and the hours can be long. However, landing a job should not be ignored. People receive up to $45,000 per year at this level, lifting them above the Federal Poverty line, providing much-needed benefits, and making enough money to exceed the Black Median Household income of $41,361. To progress to the next level, they will need to up-level themselves and invest in a Profitable Resume™.

The third level is Career. At this level, people enjoy more disposable income, time flexibility, and individuals have identified their industry niche. Generally, individuals here are known for a specific functional skillset. For example, I started my career in Human Resources as a recruiter. At this level, individuals earn up to $89,000 annually and begin to position themselves for a six-figure salary. However, people need more than a Profitable Resume™ at this stage; they need a plan. Specifically, a strategic blueprint to stop having interviews and start having confident conversations. To support this strategy, I recommend individuals to find a trusted colleague in leadership or invest in a career coach to help them along the way.

The fourth level is Career Brand, my favorite. At this stage, the most transformation happens for my clients. Not only do individuals have a greater level of career confidence, but it is also where many cross the six-figure threshold making up to $135,000. This level is vital from an emotional standpoint because researchers found $105,000 is the point in the United States, where individuals not only feel happy but are satisfied with their life choices. At this stage, individuals generally have a trusted circle of friends and advisors, including business mentors, financial professionals, and others, to help them keep growing and moving forward.

Next, we have the Boss level. At this level, individuals are generally not doing much administrative work because they can access teams and resources. These individuals enjoy high levels of flexibility and time freedom in their jobs and businesses. Typically, their salary begins at $180,000 a year. At this stage, I recommend creating a 3-year strategic legacy plan focused on your future goals and purpose.

Finally, the last level is Career Freedom. People here have full autonomy of their day and financial security where they are not concerned about bills and money. At this level, individuals are hitting over $200,000 and heading towards the top 1% of family income earners at $421,929. The next step would be to move to step two in creating a living legacy.

While I know we just went through a lot of information, the key is to read it and apply it. You should now have enough information to take action right now and assess your career freedom gap. You can go to www.findingcareerfreedom.com to get more detailed information and download a printable copy to customize. Take the time to start plotting your current position now compared to where you want to be. I focused a lot on salary ranges because people are often unaware of their career value at work. You can begin designing your future and living legacy right now. You do not have to wait for a particular time to get started in the future when you feel you have everything together. The perfect time to get started is today, right now.

If you find yourself ignoring the action points so far or hesitating to move forward, it is quite natural. It has been my experience that most people do not just need information and strategies. They need a shift in their thinking. Far too often, it is our beliefs and mindsets which block success. However, please do not be ashamed or alarmed; this happens to the best of us, including me! But once I knew better, I did better. And now YOU know better, so it is time to grow.

Belief is the mind's attitude, and your mind can be a positive supercomputer or be a weapon of mass destruction. Disbelief is defined as having the wrong attitude. But what it boils down to is a lack of trust, specifically self-trust. A lack of confidence in yourself to believe you are qualified to do what you want to do. It is entirely understandable because life has provided numerous stories and examples where you may feel like a failure or feel ill-equipped to handle the task in front of you. But let us be clear, there is a BIG difference between FEELING like a failure and FAILING BY GIVING UP. Three tips I recommend helping shift into a positive mindset are:

1. Feeding yourself positivity. If you have negative thinking patterns or are surrounded by naysayers, I recommend listening to messages from Goalcast for inspiration and encouragement. You are going to have to replace the negative thoughts with positive ones.
2. Find a community of like-minded people focused on personal and professional development for support. If you are struggling to stay positive, this would not be the best time to be alone with your thoughts. As the founder of National Black Man Day™, I invite you to join our

community because I think we are pretty awesome (but I am biased). However, many other notable organizations can support you on your journey.

3. Create an action plan for success. Incorporate this into your daily routine, so you can see yourself growing and working towards success.

For over a decade, my story has encouraged others. Honestly, I do not aim to be an inspiration. I have just chosen to lead and live my life in a way where anything is possible. Not just for myself, but for anyone who has access to me.

The power to achieve career freedom and start living your legacy resides in you, but resilience is required. Being resilient is not just a catchphrase; it is who I am. When you have been fired from your career and your business, had to face eviction and foreclosure, and watch the ones you love lying in hospital beds as I have, you realize life is what YOU make it, the good, the bad, AND the ugly.

My legacy begins with me, and today your gift starts anew. So instead of wishing, hoping, and praying away your situation, take action! Start creating your living legacy by taking the next step by visiting www.findingcareerfreedom.com to download and customize your plan. Once there, you will get access to additional resources to support you along the way. Remember that building a worthwhile legacy is not a sprint. It is a marathon.

* * *

To learn more by enrolling in Dr. Ashley's masterclass, point your cell phone's camera at the QR code then click the link:

MATTIE
DEED

Mattie is a Boston resident surrounded by her three awesome daughters, grandchildren, sisters, brother and friends. If you remembers nothing else, please know that she is kind, compassionate, patient and passionate about helping culturally, economically and socially diverse individuals to connect with occupational skills training, career ladders employment opportunities, financial empowerment tools, budgeting to saving and establishing credit by any natural or spiritual means necessary!

With over 24 years in Workforce Development Services, partnering with community-based organizations to meet the needs of job seekers of all background and circumstances, Mattie specializes in assisting clients with goals, resume and cover letter writing, interviewing skills, online job applications, mock interviews, networking, social media, financial empowerment, budgeting, credit building / debt resolution and much more. Mattie is an accomplished leader with extensive experience in the non-profit sector and assisted in the creation and development of Boston's first One-Stop Career Center (The Work Place, 1995), the MOSES (Massachusetts One-Stop Employment Systems), the Roxbury Resource Center (1998) and the Allston/Brighton Resource Center (2006.

Mattie is also a Spoken Word Artist. Her first book, "Fourth Realm: Where All Things Are Possible" was published in 2005. She is currently writing her second book which focuses on workforce development, job search strategies, and financial coaching. She is a member of the Library of International Poetry and a former member of the "57" Writers and Readers Group of Allston/Brighton" where her poetry is published in their writings.

Mattie holds a Bachelor's Degree in Human Resource Management, University of Massachusetts Boston and holds an Associate Degree in Office Management from Newbury College; she is a Notary Public and has a Certificate of Completion in Financial Coaching! Mattie fellowships with St John Missionary Baptist Church since 1969 where she created the only Workforce Development Ministry!

CONTACT:

Email: deed02119@netscape.net

Phone: 617-224-6803

Social Media: @MattieDeed

MAKE YOUR *Credit* MATTER!

Writing this chapter in this anthology has been a dream and work in progress for many years. This idea was birthed out of my desire in 1991, when I entered my first workforce development position. I was working as a Career Counselor working with ethnically and culturally diverse individuals who were laid off due to plant closings around Massachusetts.

Growing up in a large family, I was the youngest of 11. Our beloved, strong, mother, Marie Howard-Deed, was the successful head of maintaining a 500-acre farm. She taught me my first financial literacy lesson, "when you get a dime save a nickel." She expressed the importance of saving for a rainy day. Now do not get me wrong, a dime during the 50's was worth lots of money. When we went to the store, we were able to make purchases and get change back. Money had value and our mother made sure we knew it. This was my first lesson on the importance of saving money to travel to Boston in search of a better life.

In today's economy in Massachusetts, and especially during a pandemic, income can come from many different sources. It can come from wages earned (taxable income), financial gifts, unemployment benefits, stimulus income, pandemic relief, SNAP benefits, part-time employment, rental income, business ownership, income from a family member, investments and/or other financial gifts, Social Security Disability Income, Social Security Retirement Income, Child Support Payments, TAFDC, and Lottery Winnings. The sources of income are endless.

Now when we think about income, it is so important to think about budgeting, spending, and saving. These are especially important decisions. Whether you get paid weekly or bi-weekly, look at this income monthly, and create a monthly budget. This budget becomes the spending and savings guide. We must create an opportunity for saving money especially during a time of pandemic and uncertainty. Our nation is experiencing challenges in the changing of leadership and COVID-19 is on an upward spike. It is an important period of constant change in our financial environment. A time of reckoning is at hand and decisions are being made about whether to increase the stimulus payments to all. We must look at how we are spending our hard-earned money, fixed income, stimulus checks, pandemic relief, and handling rental and mortgage arrears payments.

I mentioned these benefits because as a Financial Coach, my role is to empower my clients to take charge of their finances and commit to their financial obligations. It is critical for me to be knowledgeable about other financial resources within the community and how to access them as the needs arises. When incomes drop, we seek out financial resources to bridge the income gap. We create a monthly budget to look at income vs. expenses to determine the monthly net income, (this is the money that will determine whether how much we can save or not). We know that many expenses are fixed and must be paid on time each month i.e., rent/mortgage, utilities, phone, car payment, car insurance, auto gas and MBTA Transportation Monthly Pass. There may be some variable cost along the way, these include groceries, laundry/dry cleaning, internet/cable, computer access (this is becoming a virtual necessity to conducting job search, interviewing, submitting resumes online, etc.). Monthly expenses can include virtual media, i.e., Zoom, Google Meet, FaceTime to easily connect with professionals in a certain field, for monthly meetings, and working remotely with our clients during one-one financial coaching.

We must hold fast to spending no more than what we can afford, saving as a goal in creating a good healthy credit score. Now I want to shift and talk about the credit FICO Score. The FICO score is critical to obtaining low interest loans, i.e., mortgages, auto loans, student loans and purchasing a car! Having a spending plan is also critical to taking family vacation or being able to purchase the holiday and birthday gifts we want to give to family, friends, monthly tithing, and offerings.

We must be able to set our minds on what is reasonable when spending and making on time monthly payments when it comes to credit. If you have a revolving credit card, always maintain 70% of the 100% credit limit. This means that you only spend 30% of your credit limit. Keeping your availability at 70% will ensure that your credit score will increase and never decrease. When the monthly invoice for your credit card is due, do not delay, pay it right away. When you pay on time, your credit FICO Score increases. I guarantee you that by the end of one year your credit FICO Score will be at a maximum of 600 plus.

One of my clients came in to meet with me 2 years ago, his goal was to purchase a home in 2 years. I was convinced that this was going to take place just as he spoke it, but first we had to improve his Credit FICO Score. It was not a good score; so, we did a couple of things. First, we agreed that he would open a secure credit card account with a new bank, apply for the TWIN Account pay down his lowest debts first, using the snowball affects; pay a debt off then take that money and add it to the second debt until it's paid off and so on and so forth. When he followed the action plan we created, by April 2020, he purchased his dream home: 5 huge bedrooms with 2 walk-in closets, 2 huge full baths, huge front, and back yard. He is also up for a management position within his company. He lives 20 minutes away from his new job location. He is one of many of my success stories for reporting to our funders.

The Score is where it is at and can look like this!! Let us look at it!

300-549 = Poor (F)

550-579 = Satisfactory Unsatisfactory (D to C-)

580-619 = Above Satisfactory (B- to B+)

620-729 = Good (B+ to A+)

680-750 = Very Good (A+)

751 or Higher = Excellent (A++)

SOLUTIONS TO MAINTAINING YOUR GOOD CREDIT SCORE:

1. Make on time payments by automating payments for your bills account.
2. Pay down your debt! Especially credit cards. Get the balance below 30% of the credit limit.
3. Piggyback. Become an authorized user!
4. Pay off with pennies and make your credit "Jump like Jack Flash".
5. Use secure credit cards.
6. Try not to co-sign for anything, if you do, do a co-signer release or refinance the loan.

Keep in mind also that the Credit Score has these 5 Components~~

- 10% Inquiries (these are the hard pulls when financial lenders pull your credit
- 10% Type of Debt
- 15% Length of Credit History (do not take off credit history, this cost you something
- 30% Debt-to-Income-Ratio
- 35% Payment History (it is so important to pay bills monthly and on time).

Negative information reports older than two years does not highly affect your FICO Score the newest stuff makes the most impression the FICO Score. The FICO Score measures weather a person is moving towards or away from bankruptcy; all your creditors can cancel your credit cards or increase your interest rates when you are late on any of these accounts. Your credit is your financial GPA.

Now if we are to get the most out of your money to secure your future, we are to build a create a budget that reflects your monthly income, all your expenses for that month, and hopefully at the end you have a positive net income. My clients when we are working together after they create the monthly budget; I purposefully provide them with a copy of the budget and discuss their spending with them, we look at needs vs wants and see where we can cut back on expenses. It is amazing when we do it together, it becomes a much more user-friendly process and the elephant in the room is just nothing more than a mouse! We reduce cash outflow so much that they see a huge difference and feel financial relief immediately.

During a pandemic, we are not eating out, we are not taking expensive vacations, we are not making trips to the hair salons and resorts, spas, and other pleasures we are no longer privy to! We are excited about financial literacy because it can be applied, and we see immediate results with our finances.

This positive net income is what we going to work with in terms of savings. Before I mentioned savings, we must talk about emergency savings. We want to make sure that we have several savings pockets. One savings can be created specifically for a family vacation when COVID-19 allows it. A second savings can be an emergency fund for meeting rent or other utilities when income drops. The third savings is more long term to purchase a home.

An important step to home buying is to increase your FICO Score to 750+. I mentioned increasing your credit score to pay your bills on time which means only charging what you need. Having one credit card account or having one revolving secure credit card account can be utilized in most places you shop. This credit card will allow you to manage your spending and make monthly payments on time. The next step in home buying would be to make sure that you have a savings plan where you are putting money aside on a monthly basis every year. This type of savings can take time, sometimes up to three years but nonetheless you must maintain an aggressive saving plan. Once you have saved a sizable down payment for your home, take the homebuying class through a reputable source either NAACA, Boston Home Center or through other community-based organizations.

I want to go back another important thing about saving, make sure you pay yourself after you pay all the bills. We cannot go out and spend money without saving money. If you dream it, you can plan it and you can have it. What do I mean by this? Be conscious of your finances doing the pandemic. How we spend affects our peace of mind.

My dear beloved mother, Marie Howard-Deed called it, "keeping your hands open". She explained this concept in terms of having open hands. She told us, "when your hands are open, you can give, and you can receive." Someone else said, "it is better to give than to receive." However, we know when to give of our finances and when not to, because you can only give what you have.

I am reminded of an area in the Bible where this poor widow woman who gave her last 2 copper coins. She gave in faith and this means there is a higher value placed on making sacrifices with our finances when we do it from our heart. Some have extraordinarily little during this pandemic due to lost jobs, incomes, rent increases, mortgages falling behind, along with so many other things; food became an issue of insecurities. The bare necessities have been limited. Stores limited the number of paper items consumers could purchase. COVID-19 taught us the value of living a humble, frugal life.

Our finances dropped and we were encouraged to live a different lifestyle while having our basic needs met. When it comes tor money, I am of the mindset that God has made us stewards over our finances. We make sacrificial offerings when we budget and live within our means. Now let us not get it twisted. This means, while living on a budget, we are still able to eat out ocassionaly and enjoy healthy foods. Foods that are less healthy can cost greatly when we are trying ot save. We veer off to fulfilling wants, more than needs. Every time you are considering a new purchase—be it furniture, a cellphone, a computer, or a remodeled bathroom—ask yourself if you getting what is necessary to meet a need or want? Is there a less expensive option available? During difficult times, our goals should be to spend as little as possible to fulfill our needs.

When we live below our means but within our needs, we also set ourselves up for a substantial retirement. When I am coaching my clients, I emphasize spending on wants over needs can make the difference in receiving a return on your investment in retirement. Living on a budget, living within our means, does not mean that we do not splurge on some of the things that we enjoy. It just means that we are cautious when we spend. Working remotely has afforded us an opportunity to be budget conscious. We are no longer eating out as much. We are cooking more therefore we are cooking more healthy foods than when we were eating out. We go grocery shop with coupons. We look for more bargains when we shop online. We take our time and decide what we need from the grocery store therefore, making a grocery list before we shop. We are saving more money working from home than ever before. COVID-19 has afforded us an opportunity to save money, which is a positive thing. While it has taken a toll on others with the loss of family members

I maintain on the importance of budgeting, savings, establishing and resolving credit are crucial to your financial status. Building WEALTH is a simple equation, Assets - Liabilities = Net Worth. If purchasing a home is a goal, building credit is critical, especially for low-income households.

Always remember that your present financial circumstances do not determine where you can go, they determine where you start. Contact me right now to make YOUR Financial Empowerment Matter! I am here to serve you!

* * *

To learn more by enrolling in Mattie's masterclass, point your cell phone's camera at the QR code then click the link:

REV. ROGER
DIXON, SR.

Rev Roger E Dixon, Sr. CEO and owner or Dixon Retail HUT/Aularale Skin Care Cosmetics. He is retired and work presently as a substitute teacher. Community Leader with the youth, Prison Ministry Mentor and volunteer as a Hospital Chaplain in Harrisburg, Pennsylvania. Rev Dixon helps at risk youth in the community to reach their goals and dreams for success and serve as a mentor. Rev Dixon teaches life skills with the youth who comes from single family homes. He helps parents to understand their kids and with life struggles. There are workshops to help youth and parents.

Rev Dixon have 30 years' experience in Prison Ministry. He helps and ministers to Men and women in the prison system. He teaches life skills and help them find jobs and get their GED. There is follow up when the get out of prison. Rev Dixon have a counseling session to help follow through when they get home. Through his inspiring message Men and Women in the Community have been inspired to reach their goals. He has a podcast call "Prison Family Ministry" Facebook live.

He is the founder of Heritage Community Outreach a 501 C (3) non-profit organization that supports the youth, prison ministry, and community needs.

CONTACT:

https://thebestfive5.kartra.com/page/4secrets

MAKE YOUR *Success* MATTER!

SUCCESS IS YOURS; DO YOU WANT IT? YOU, YOU, AND EVEN YOU.

In my experience being a teacher, talking to students about education and their lives; I found that some students believe they will never be successful in life. My job is to remind them that focusing on their dreams and aspirations can help them to achieve anything. Most importantly, never allow distractions to rob you of your dreams. You see, most students do not see college or trade school in their future, as they are mostly worried about graduating and getting a job to "make ends meet". They believe they must work after school as this is the only way to survive. They share their testimonies of poverty, emphasizing that this does not only apply to the homelessness. Some students come from a single-family household where both mother and father are present; some come from cities and rural areas; some live in the suburbs. As the student population is extremely diverse, my words remain the same: "Do whatever it takes to be successful in all areas of your life.

Never give up, always stay focused on your future". In writing this chapter I cannot help but to empathize with my students. Who will help them? Nevertheless, I remind them that they can defeat their struggles by studying hard in the classroom. Also, by reminding them they are indeed successful and that they have the ability to show the world who they are.

Daily, I meet with students who believe that they will never have success in their lives. They believe that due to their background, upbringing, and popularity that they cannot push forward. In some areas we can credit the lack of support by family and friends as a reason or excuse for why they will never make it. They all have dreams and goals in some capacity; Mr. Dixon tells them, "they will prosper in education and life and to never listen to the naysayers. Mr. Dixon also reminds them, "to focus on uplifting themselves knowing that success is not out of reach. Teachers, parents, guardians, and friends, if we are concerned, we must show our children more love. It is the great foundation of true success. Faith the size of a mustard seed coupled with encouraging words and uplifting sentiments is the recipe our children need to thrive in all areas of their lives.

I like to share with my students the meaning of success and what to do with it in their adolescent years and beyond. First, we must understand success. It means different things to many people. The dictionary defines success as the feet of getting or achieving wealth, respect, or fame, the correct or desired result of an attempt. As an educator, these definitions capture the essence and objectives of success. Earl Nightingale, who is called the "Dean" of personal motivation describes success with a twist as he states "Success as the progressive relegation of a worthy goal or worthy ideal. Too many students attach the moniker of success to the result of achieving success, buying a car, gaining after school employment, becoming a millionaire, achieving material wealth. Mr. Nightingale brings a new perspective to success through the word progressive. "As long as you are progressing," he says, "towards a predetermined goal, you are in fact a success." I ask my students "How do you define success?" This is an opportunity to add ideas, insight, and guidance in their journey to achieving their own success.

I explain to my students that as you get older, you will see areas in your life that show opportunities for progress. Mr. Nightingale says, "as long as you are progressing toward a predetermined goal, you are a success." Students should remain focused and avoid distraction in such a way as to continue to progress in meeting their goals and aspirations. It has become apparent -and relatable- that students can be distracted by many things including but not limited to family, friends and negative energy around them. I encourage students to surround themselves with positivity and seek a mentor in their community. It is imperative for them to know they are valuable to society as well as themselves. In many ways, their success is everyone's success. I explain to them that when we meet new people, we must be kind because we want the same respect to be given to us.

I like to share some of the books that I read with my students in hopes to widen the spectrum of understanding success. One particular book I read stood out to me and I shared it with them. The book is "Lessons from A Third Grade Dropout" By Rick Rigsby. Dr. Rick learns from his father to be kind to everyone you meet. Kind deeds are never lost. His father repeated these words to Rick and his siblings every chance he could. The author says, "the impact of his words reflected the capacity of kindness his father possessed. Kindness is not just a word, but a way of life."

A student's success in life should be rooted in some way to their level of kindness and compassion to others. It is great to lead by example. As a teacher, I believe showing the power of kindness will enhance your life and lives of those around you. The kinder you are, the more fulfilling your life will be. In today's culture, there is a significant lack of kindness in youth and young adults. It is expected that we are taught how to treat people by our words and actions. Unfortunately, some students as well as others, do not know how to do this. To receive respect, you must show respect.

Students should know what success means to them as success is a personal experience of well-being, confidence, and accomplishment. The student should create the habit of claiming success in their own life. Whether your pursuit of success is in healthcare, business, or even in your personal life; you must find the tools necessary to make it happen. The most powerful influence in success is making a decision and committing to it. In order to thrive you must claim your success with knowledge of your goal and commitment to achieve it. Students are all faced with choices, large or small in their lifetime. If you choose to be happy, then you must understand what makes you happy. If you choose to be successful, you must understand what it takes for you to be successful. As Abraham Lincoln states "Are most folks as happy as they make up their minds to be?".

Students should know that their level of success indicates how willing they were to help others to reach their level of success. It is important for students to have a mentor to follow to be able to recognize such clues. Mentors who have reached their own level of success are able to provide guidance in how to live your own life to your fullest potential, or "Slam Dunk Success" if you will. Just as you can build relationships with your teammates on the courts, the same can be done with the coach. In most cases, the coach is experienced and very well versed in the game of basketball; able to provide knowledge and wisdom to each play helping you to finesse them. This takes a "pay it forward attitude" on the coach's end to ensure success in his or her team. My own personal success was not achieved without coaches and mentors who believed I was greater than I settled to be; I was taught this through books, seminars, workshops, and coaching.

The takeaway from this chapter is that success is yours if you want it. You must make things happen to achieve your own level of success. This may require one or more role models, mentors, and well-versed people in your life willing to help you manifest your hopes and dreams. You must claim your success and confirm the answers to the following questions.

- What is it that you want to achieve?
- What skills are necessary to achieve this goal?
- What changes in my attitude must I take on?
- What new habits and discipline are necessary?
- Are you ready to play at "Slam Dunk Level"?

Success is yours; do you want it? You, you, and even you! What does it take to make it happen? Self-Discipline change of mindset, willingness for discipline, ability to grow beyond standards. It takes drive to break from bad habits that we all have in our lives. But we as teachers, mentors, parents, and community leaders can help students reach their level of success. So, let's do it! Success is yours, claim it.

* * *

To learn more by enrolling in Roger's masterclass, point your phone's camera at the QR code then click the link:

DR. KATRINA

FERGUSON

Katrina Ferguson delivers a passionate, enthusiastic and entertaining message to both teach and encourage you to celebrate your individuality and breakthrough to become your 'greater self.' Her inspiring message is based upon lessons learned in her own breakthrough journeys. Ms. Ferguson is committed to helping others across the world apply these principles in their individual lives and relationships. In her unique, uncompromising style, she brings life changing principles and leadership skills to inspire and motivate thousands across age, gender and industry lines.

Featured in national publications, including Essence Magazine and USA Today, Ms. Ferguson has been the subject of numerous articles and interviews and her story is currently being used all over the country to train and motivate sales forces of both public and private organizations. She routinely shares the stage with company presidents and executives as she conducts trainings and presentations around the country. She has spoken for several faith-based organizations including the Potter's House in Dallas, Texas and Evangel Cathedral in Upper Marlboro, Maryland.

Ms. Ferguson speaks from her experience and success in the traditional corporate fields of real estate, financial services and law, as well as her success as an entrepreneur having owned and operated several successful businesses; experience major success in both the network marketing and publishing industries.

CONTACT:

Website: www.KatrinaFerguson.com

Email: Katrina@KatrinaFerguson.com

MAKE YOUR *Why* MATTER!

Goal setting. Two words that strike fear in the hearts of even the most accomplished strong men. How often we set out to achieve something and find that somewhere along the way, we get sidetracked, sideswiped, swindled or for whatever reason, we do not achieve them.

With all that I have accomplished, and sometimes accomplished simply means completed, there has been a key that has driven me to completion over incompletion; from an unfinished work to a finished work. That key is simply understanding the purpose and the destiny of the thing that I am writing or involved in creating.

"Always remember, if your why is big enough, the how will take care of itself."

Finally, brothers, whatever is true, whatever is honorable, whatever is just, whatever is pure, whatever is lovely, whatever is commendable, if there is any excellence, if there is anything worthy of praise, thing about these things. Philippians 4:8 (ESV)

Hot does not even begin to describe the weather on this particular Independence Day. The sweltering heat of July was thick and muggy. The dense humidity felt as if you were walking through a steam room or maybe even the jungle. As heavy as the air was, her heart was heavier. At the time, her children were fifteen, fourteen, and seven years of age. Although she faced one of the most difficult seasons of her life, she had done a good job of hiding her pain. Putting on a positive face was important since her daughters looked to her for strength, guidance, and motherly wisdom.

Independence Day . . . how ironic.

That particular day, the drive home seemed longer than normal, as every stop light seemed perfectly timed to prevent her from reaching their home. Road construction seemed to pop up instantaneously. This holiday was not as joyous as some of the others had been. Not because of the meaning of Independence Day, but because of the direction her life seemed to be going. The sky darkened long before dusk as storm clouds blotted out the sun and put a slight chill in the air. As suddenly as the temperature dropped, so did the rain . . . and her tears. Her oldest daughter noticed but did not dare to ask why her mother wept. She was old enough to pick up on the context clues and realized that life as they knew it was about to change.

Independence Day . . . how ironic.

The closer they got to the family home, the more her heart rate increased. By the time she finally pulled into the long driveway, she was on the verge of hyperventilating. God seemed to be sending down rain with fury as the large, heavy raindrops pounded against the windshield with the same speed and intensity of the tears leaving her eyes. Her thoughts raced like the winds of the storms. There were to be no fireworks on this day, at least none in the skies. The storm made sure of that.

Independence Day . . . how ironic.

The goal was to celebrate fifty years of marriage with him. As she sat there sobbing outside their home, she knew that would not be their reality. There is a saying that time will either promote you or expose you. That not only goes for people; it also goes for relationships. She tried. Really, she did. Irreconcilable differences are . . . well . . . irreconcilable. There were only two real choices. She could continue down this dead-end street, unhappy and unfulfilled, risking her self-confidence while nullifying every lesson she had taught her girls about what a relationship built on love and trust should look like, or she could leave the relationship and hope for a do over.

Despite having Biblical grounds for divorce, she never intended to leave. She had done everything she could to make it work. She fasted, prayed, and sought counseling . . . everything. That Fourth of July, she learned a lesson that would follow her for the rest of her life. The lesson was although God answers prayers, He would never go against the will of one man to answer the prayers of another. We all have a right to our own will. Our choice is between God's perfect will for our lives and His permissive will. All we can do is trust that whatever happens, God will use it for our good.

Independence Day . . . how ironic.

You may be asking yourself how I know so much about how she felt in the midst of the challenges she faced. I know because I am the woman. This was one of the most difficult seasons in my life; one I thought I would never get through. What I found though, was that this was one of my most tremendous times of growth. We have all heard it, said that "if it does not kill you, it makes you stronger." This was a strength-building season in my life. The days, weeks, months, and years to follow would present many other challenges that would strengthen me as well. Reminding myself that these seasons are just moments of time, in time. Keeping in mind that these seasons do not last forever, just as winter eventually turns to spring, allows us to go through them more gracefully. Just remember, the seasons come to pass. That is their design. There is a beginning and praise the Lord, there is also an end.

Through all the challenging seasons of my life, I discovered a foundational truth that serves as fertilizer to help you grow through every difficult situation. This wisdom separates kings from paupers, the successful from the unsuccessful. This wisdom can cause anyone to achieve the success that they desire. That piece of wisdom is simply your *WHY*, getting an understanding of *WHY* you were created. A clearly defined *WHY* will help you know your God-breathed purpose. God had something specific in mind for every one of us before the beginning of time, a definitive problem for us to solve. Our journey through this life is to discover His purpose and plan for our lives and ultimately live it. Being clear about that purpose or WHY will serve as an anchor in the turbulent waters of our journey.

Knowing *WHY* you were created is more important than knowing your name. Your reasons for doing something come first. The answers come later. If you are clear about your *WHY*, then the path to success is easier to find and follow, even when it gets rough. Your *WHY* is to your life what fuel is to a rocket. It blasts you into the future, in the direction that you need to move in to obtain absolute fulfillment and success. The key freedoms that we crave, freedom to do what we choose with our time and money will only become evident as we get crystal clear about WHY we were created in the first place.

Being clear on my *WHY* meant that as the challenges continued to come forward, I focused on finding a way through them without losing sight of who I was created to be. I have built all the success in my life around this principle and have taught others all around the world to do the same. What that means is this: if your *"WHY"* is big enough, if your *"WHY"* is strong enough, if your *"WHY"* is huge enough, then how to do that thing will take care of itself.

Unfortunately (or fortunately, depending on how you look at it), knowing your WHY does not mean that your journey to success will always be easy, just that it will be worth it. It means that what you are going through, you can actually grow through so that ultimately your greatness will show through. It is totally up to you. When you realize that your decision to pursue your *WHY* is greater than any of the circumstances of your life, you will take everything that happens in stride, simply as part of the process of your growth and development, and will work together with all the other circumstances of your life to bring you to your goal. Without a BIG WHY, small obstacles are seemingly insurmountable. With a big *WHY*, the large obstacles become absolutely invisible. What this means is "if your *WHY* is big enough, the hows will take care of themselves."

For me, my *WHY* was my kids. I have added to my *WHY*, but my family has always been the foundation that made me get out of bed and push toward my goals, even when I did not feel like doing so. As I grew through what I was going through (a success tip), I began to look at how and *WHY* I was created and what it was that God wanted from my life. I studied the Bible to determine who I was in Christ, since the creator of a thing is the best resource for information about how the thing works or should work. Dr. Myles Munroe says that "if you don't know the use of a thing, abuse is inevitable." In the process of finding my purpose, there were several *"WHY"* Wisdom Keys that helped me along the journey. Prayerfully, they will help you as well.

"WHY" Wisdom Key No. 1: Successful people have a BIG WHY that causes them to do what is necessary, even when they do not feel like it.

"But watch yourselves lest your hearts be weighed down with dissipation and drunkenness and cares of this life, and that day come upon you suddenly like a trap. For it will come upon all who dwell on the face of the whole earth. But stay awake at all times, praying that you may have strength to escape all these things that are going to take place, and to stand before the Son of Man."
~ Luke 21:34-36 (ESV)

When I speak of successful people, I am speaking of success on your own terms; however, it is that you measure success. Even after the breakup of my family, I have continued to have my fair share of challenges and opportunities for growth. Through it all, I have kept my *WHY* in front of me. Of course, as the kids grew and their needs changed, so has my *WHY*. A clue to your *WHY* is "What Hurts You?" In other words, what touches you so deeply that it makes you cry to think about not achieving it? What is the problem that you were created to solve, the problem that moves you at the core of your being? What gives you pain in the pit of your stomach or a lump in your throat when you think about disappointing those waiting for you to get yourself together and live your destiny?

For some, those emotions stop them rather than driving them enough to make things happen. For the successful person, this becomes their motivation, their inspiration, to keep going. As an alternative acronym for *WHY*, try "What Helps You?" What helps you get out of bed early and stay up late working toward your goals? What helps you go the extra mile and do a better job than is expected? What helps you become more so that you can have more and do more?

Choosing a faith-based *WHY*, rather than a fear-based WHY is a much more powerful position. Rather than being scared to action, you are moving forward in an inspired and enlightened state. Choose faith over fear.

"WHY" Wisdom Key No. 2: Successful people use adversity as fuel to propel them to their goals.

"Not that I have already obtained this or am already perfect, but I press on to make it my own, because Christ Jesus has made me his own."
~ Philippians 3:12 (ESV)

Many people use challenges and adversities as the reasons they cannot succeed. The reason that you think you cannot be successful should be the reason that you must be successful. For instance, many use their children as their excuse for failing when their children should be the reason *WHY* they must succeed. My children were my *WHY* and a very *BIG WHY* at that. At first, it was all about survival. The bare necessities were my main priority since I had to do things on my own. The happy little family I had envisioned for myself was no more, and it was time for me to accept my season as a single parent and move toward my goals with speed and boldness. While balancing work, kids, activities, and church, I continued to look for a better way. Something about eating was important to them, so I had to figure out a way to feed them.

Living just above the poverty level did not sit well with me. Knowing that God had a bigger plan for my life, I set out to find out what it was while providing for my children and doing what was necessary to create a life for us all.

"WHY" Wisdom Key No. 3: Successful people do what they must do now so that ultimately, they can have and do what they desire.

"If anyone would come after me, let him deny himself and take up his cross daily and follow me."
~ Luke 9:23 (ESV)

Up until the separation, I was a stay-at-home mom. Our house was the Kool-Aid house where my kids' friends came to play. As a result of the shift in my life, I had to do something to meet our basic needs. Even though I had great aspirations of becoming a successful businessperson, I had to start somewhere so that we were not hungry. A job became a starting place to solve our problems. Boy was I glad that my start did not dictate my finish. The job was an okay place to start, but I knew it was not where I was going to finish. Walking into a building every day that did not have my name on it, being paid what someone else said I was worth, working when they told me to work, taking off when they permitted me to do so meant I was building someone else's dream while my dream lay dormant. My *WHY* was the key to me pursuing my dream of becoming a successful business owner, featured in magazines, and rubbing shoulders with some of the most prolific minds and speakers of our time.

"WHY" Wisdom Key No. 4: Successful people never ever give up on their dreams, yet they do separate themselves from negative thinking, people, and habits.

"Now faith is the assurance of things hoped for, the conviction of things not seen."
~ Hebrews 11:1 (ESV)

"In the same way, let your light shine before others, so that they may see your good works and give glory to your Father who is in heaven."
~ Matthew 5:16 (ESV)

People sometimes look at my life now and think that it was easy for me. The houses, cars, vacations, and multiple streams of income—they all came with a price. There have been many more businesses fail than have been successful. Part of the process is to learn from what does not work so that you do not continually make errors in judgment. Additionally, you cannot allow your past to dictate your future. It is so easy to have pity parties when things are not going your way.

That Fourth of July, I could have simply given up on life. I could have settled for a meager existence and been on welfare for the rest of my life. Please do not misunderstand; I am not saying that public assistance is a bad thing. You would be surprised at the number of successful people in the world that have had to get help in order to survive at some point in their lives. When it becomes a way of life, however, and you are given money and resources without having to work for them, it can negatively affect your mental well-being, your self-esteem, and your confidence. The programs were designed to assist the public during challenging financial seasons, not as a way of life.

My grandmother said, "A closed mouth does not get fed." Do not be too proud to get the help you need in the season that you need it. Just do not allow it to become the crutch that dulls your intellect and kills your drive. Pride often keeps us from allowing others to help us. Scripture says that "pride goes before destruction." Use the help to position yourself to help others. Charity is a two-way street. Moreover, if you find yourself falling, as my good friend Les Brown always says, "Fall on your back because if you can look up, you can get up."

"WHY" Wisdom Key No. 5: Successful people distract themselves from their distractions.

"So let's keep focused on that goal, those of us who want everything God has for us. If any of you have something else in mind, something less than total commitment, God will clear your blurred vision - you'll see it yet!"
~ Hebrews 12:15(ESV)

Obstacles are what you see when you take your eyes off your goal. Any obstacle that stands in the way of your moving toward your goal is a distraction. Most of the time, distractions are neither good nor bad; they tend to be things, habits, or people that we consistently allow to interfere with our forward movement. Successful people distract themselves from their distractions. There is always a way to achieve your goals and dreams! Find it. If you cannot find it, make it. Continue moving forward at all costs; your *WHY* depends on it.

Yes, what you love is a clue to your purpose and your destiny. It is also a clue to where you will find your greatest resistance. Expect it. Often our way through the distractions of our lives is about reevaluating what we are giving priority status in our lives. Some relationships, some jobs, social media, even our children can be distracting us from who God intended us to be and who He intended for us to bless. Some of us need to cut the information umbilical cord and turn off the television and the Internet. Watching television takes you out of your own life and into someone else's. One of my mentors calls television the electronic income reducer. Stop watching others tell you their vision and work on your own. Remember, focus is crucial to our process, and what we focus on expands. No matter what goes on around us, we must give it minimal attention so that we keep our goal destination in sight.

"Therefore, since we are surrounded by so great a cloud of witnesses, let us also lay aside every weight, and sin which clings so closely, and let us run with endurance the race that

is set before us, looking to Jesus, the founder and perfecter of our faith, who for the joy that was set before him endured the cross, despising the shame, and is seated at the right hand of the throne of God."
~ Hebrews 12:1-2 (ESV)

It is very difficult for me to give you everything you need in life to be prosperous in this short chapter. Success comes from a combination of thoughts and actions. What I do know for sure is that knowing your *WHY*—your reason for being—is one of the most important variables for your success. There must be a strong enough reason *WHY* you want to succeed. There must be something that gives you the necessary energy to keep going when all the odds are against you. We all have one thing in common: a *BIG WHY* will move you in the directions that will bring fulfillment into your life and the lives of others that you touch through your actions. Whatever you do, find your WHY and fly. Live a life so powerful that people will want to read your story and point to you as an example of greatness!

EXERCISE

Have you figured out your *WHY*? If you were already clear on your WHY, maybe it's time to renew it. Write yourself a letter. Start it by saying how much you love yourself; we do not tell ourselves that enough. Then begin to write your *WHY*. Why do you need to be successful? Who are the people in your life that you have to become the best version of "you" to support? Is there something in your heart that keeps you awake at night dreaming of the possibilities for your life? Is there a cause that you can get behind and work toward to make the world a better place? Everybody reading this may have a different answer, yet we will all have a *WHY*. Once you have written the letter, put it somewhere where you can see it often. It will serve as a reminder and inspiration for you to stay the course of living on purpose and doing destiny.

If you would like to connect with me, send me your letter

by e-mail to Katrina@KatrinaFerguson.com. It would be my pleasure to offer you some assistance and a free tool that will assist you on your journey to becoming your greater self. Also, visit my website at *www.KatrinaFerguson.com* for even more resources to assist you.

* * *

To learn more by enrolling in Dr. Katrina's masterclass, point your cell phone's camera at the QR code then click the link:

JUANITA H.
GRANT

Parent Mastermind creator and thought leader, Juanita H. Grant knows empowerment is key to making lasting change in people's lives. Through her Inspire by Juanita platform she provides a safe space for parents to share resources and be better providers and nurturers for their children without losing their mind or their sanity. Over the last 20 years Juanita has fostered 25 children, two of which she went on to fully adopt.

Hailing from Boston, MA, Juanita is a transformational speaker, who champions parent and youth intervention including substance abuse and suicide prevention. Her passion for parents and children led her to develop the Parent Mastermind where participants do a deep dive into foundational practices of powerful parenting. For years she has worked in the trenches to help Parents get unstuck and pave the way for a brighter future for themselves and their children.

Juanita's other special interests include Business and Life Coaching, Vision Boarding, Financial Literacy, Urban Ministries and Theology. She is currently a doctoral candidate at Global University Christian Exchange and has a Master's of Science in Community Economic Development from Southern New Hampshire University.

CONTACT:

Website: Inspirebyjuanita.org

Email: inspirebyjuanita@gmail.com

Phone: 617-955-1207

MAKE YOUR

MATTER!

Never in my life, did I ever think that things in my past would really matter or even make an impact. Why? Because I never really understood that I really mattered. No one ever knew that inner child inside of me felt that way. I lived with memories that did not line up with who I am today. As a Parent, I knew from experience that everything I did must be intentional and different so that my children will not grow up replaying life's torments over in their mind like the skipping CD that was scratched by a negligent person who handled it carelessly.

In life, you will find everything that you do, that you touch, and that you speak out of your mouth is impactful and it leaves footprints in the hearts of those we encounter in life daily! I have worked hard over the years to be the best at what I do. If nothing else, it was my desire to be a better parent than my mother and father were to me.

Seven days, 8 hours, and 53 minutes old. So beautiful, My first grandchild: Light skin, head full of jet-black hair, deep blue no grey eyes, and that dimple in your left cheek. 10 fingers, 10 toes, 2 arms, 2 legs, everything in its place, perfection once again. As I sit down and gaze into your eyes, I see the seed that was planted years ago when I had my first-born child at 6:18 pm. It was on a cold January 16 that he entered this world. The doctors monitored the equipment in the room, the nurses made sure that I was comfortable, the father of my child, my mother, aunt, and others waited in anticipation for my son to come out after I carried him for nine long months. Forced labor pains, with medicine coming from an IV to induce me, just to push him out naturally, your right, no medication for pain, not an easy task! In fact, I will never forget that pain! I thank God for my man son who today, January 15th has a daughter now, so beautiful.

According to, *www.psychologytoday.com, most parents work to give children the best start possible, but it is also important for parents to recognize that kids come into the world with their own temperaments, personalities and goals. While parents may want to push their children down a certain path, a parent's job is to provide and interface with the world that ultimately prepares a child for complete independence and the ability to pursue what ever path they choose.*

Parenting never came with instructions, nor rules to the game. The truth is who said we needed to have all the answers? However, many of us did the best we could for our children, some did well with it and others did not even know where to begin. Many of us wanted to be better parents then our parents were to us.

Providing a safe space for parents that includes grandparents, foster, adoptive, and spiritual, to share resources, be better providers and nurtures for our children. Without losing our mind or our sanity. Initially, Inspire by Juanita was birthed in 2015. I decided to share some things and be real. Transparency has never been easy for me; it was because of what I experienced from adolescence. This was the gateway for what I experienced to show that I was not always perfect. That I was just simply learning day by day. I was learning wisdom, with the world as my parents. My heartbeat in my chest like never before. When I stood on stage talking to over 300 people. I believe as parents we must take care of ourselves 1st. when our wellbeing is all set, we can nurture our families to the full. If you want to get your sanity back, after today, make sure you connect with me to learn more about what Parent Mastermind, through Inspired by Juanita has to offer you! Today I am happy, a single mother of four, two biological man sons, two adoptive teenagers and an amazing foster parent to a beautiful young lady. I am an author and speaker, excited to say that my mom and I are building a good, healthy relationship but it was not always this way!

When I got violated, I felt that it was all my fault. It took time for me to heal from the pain that was inside of me. It takes wise people to talk with you, to remind you that you were not in a decision-making capacity. It is not your fault when someone is attacking you with different things, such as abuse, molestation, bullying or neglect. You were not mature to fully understand why this had happened to you. You might not have thought it through but somewhere deep down, its constantly gnaws at you. Your mind is closed, when you find true love, and he can see what happened in the past was not your fault, can you be opened to let him in or allow your past to hinder an amazing future? We want to be changed; true love can come when you are least expected. Do not allow confusion of spirits cloud your judgement for love, true love and true understanding with God's help you are able to open now and become transparent to be able to show people the real you.

How do you explain as a child being only 12 years old, that you were raped in a locker room? The evidence showed when I found out that I was six and a half months pregnant and experienced an abortion once it was revealed, because I was a minor, someone else made a choice for me, that went against everything that I believed. I wanted to end my life right after that because I felt like I did not protect my daughter who I held in my arms after delivering her shortly after my 13th birthday. I was looked down on by my family and I was told that I would never be anything in my life. I transferred to a new school and I was preyed upon as fresh meat, with no family, or friends to stand by me. I was bullied in school, jumped and beat often because, I was an attractive young lady while my self-esteem was at its lowest.

This led me to become an over achiever in life and I worked hard to make sure that I did everything right. I was very protective of my children when I had them because I felt God was giving me another opportunity after the loss of my first daughter. I felt I had to love them, as both a mother and father because their father left us and married the woman, he cheated on me with. Leaving me to raise our children alone, as we discussed several times that was not my desire.

At the end of 2015, after completing a program for local parents, I made the decision to open my life to the world for the first time. I prayed and asked GOD to release me from the weight that held me down and ate away at me for most of my life! The little girl that cried on the inside, while the woman raised powerful Foster Children and encouraged them to be the best they could ever be! I shared the buried details from my childhood, the painful experiences that plagued me and clouded my judgement! Vulnerably I stood there, sharing where I once was broken, abused and abandoned. I shared who I was at that time, and confidently, for the first time I shared where I was headed in the future. There was not a dry eye in the whole entire auditorium.

The weight of the burden and the trauma that was hindering me personally and professionally was now lifted. I kept replaying those senses in my mind repeatedly. No one ever knew how broken I truly was. Hidden behind a captivating smile, a million-dollar strut and dressed for success. Broken!

So called friends who called me cocky. Intimidated by my new displayed confidence! Not even knowing the inside of me had holes within. The little girl who cried herself to sleep. The woman who was alone and felt lonely but not alone because HIS Angels watched over her daily.

I appeared noticeably confident growing up. I was sent to church as a child and I would go to learn about the Lord. I am incredibly grateful that my mom sent me to church at a young age. Initially, I was very resentful, it was boring as a child, but as I got older, I prayed for my mom and my family. I never thought to pray for myself. I often give thanks for her today, because that lead me to be the strong woman that I am.

From my past experiences I learned complete forgiveness. I forgave the man who took my innocence, I forgave my family who supported from a distance, after my first book, I went to lunch with my mom for the first time alone in my life. It was very awkward initially, but I was so excited the little girl within me leaped for joy! Although my siblings tried to crucify me for sharing the truth about what I had experienced. I forgave my middle school bully. When I saw her at a church event, I embraced her and let her know then I forgave her a long time ago and with tears in her eyes, she looked deep in my eyes and said, "I am sorry hurt people, hurt people."

The burden that secretly tormented me was broken on that day, my children get to see me living a life of freedom and success! Which reminds me of a young man that I mentored and who participated in my pilot program.

I will not use a name for his privacy. My client could not read, has three daughters, was locked up in jail and after working with me, he reads daily to his children, he has his barbers license now and owns his own Barber shop today. This young man has custody of his children. It is amazing to see how committed he is to help his children complete their homework daily. Our children do not come with an instruction manual.

It is not where you start, it is the journey that you go through to end up where you are supposed to be. These things could have led me to be an abusive parent. I learned to break the cycle of being abused, I chose to be nurturing, loving, caring and kind to my children. I chose to push my children to excellence; I chose to encourage my children to live better lives than most people we know.

Sometimes we are searching for our purpose in life. I always taught on finances and I helped many find their first home for their family. **We do not realize that our gift is the very thing that we do every day.** While talking to my coach, during a VIP session. I remember her saying to me, No Juanita, I do not feel you should be teaching on financing. I asked her why? Unbeknownst to me, she listened to several of my calls, speaking to my children and explaining that my trip was temporary. After she observed how I handled the repeated calls. The lightbulb went off and she exclaimed, that is it! That is your gift. I was confused. She said I see you doing a Mastermind, one for Parents. She called everyone in the room and asked what did they think? That is, it, Parent Mastermind. I was not happy with her assessment of my gift. They were full of excitement.

I wanted to get away from parenting and youth! That is what I worked with all my life. I loved children and helping them to get to a better space in life. I loved working with Parents, teaching them new skills and conversation pieces to build better bridges between themselves and their children, family and schools. I went home sad and could not think straight. I finally got it a year later. My coach was onto something! What a genius. The very thing I avoided, was the thing that everyone came to me for advice, the very thing where I found the resources for effortlessly. I thought my past did not qualify me to be a good parent, but I learned that it made me a Parent Mastermind! I know the signs of bullying, molestation, suicide, and neglect. I have experienced many things that led me to be protective of children on all levels and have a level of experience most people today just do not understand.

I have studied trauma, family dynamics, sit on the board for Mass Alliance for Families, a foster parent for over 30 children over the years. I guess I am qualified to be a Parent Mastermind.

What I tell parents today:

While you need to be a parent and not a friend but friendly, so your child feels comfortable confiding in you.

In order to be an amazing parent in the nowadays - during these uncertain times, you got to make it, really, relevant in order to be an amazing parent in 2021. 2020 was a complete change in life during this COVID-19 Pandemic time and any other times with any other things of this nature that may occur. With all the home schooling today, our children eating everything in the fridge, they are leaving the home a mess with stinky stuff in the trash and it is frustrating. In order to be an amazing parent, you must take care of yourself first. This year get up and exercise to circulate your blood start now in 2021! Do Not let COVID-19 dismantle your family or work. Parents, you must self-nurture, take a bath instead of a shower sometimes, be deliberate with breathing exercises to wind down daily. With all of life's changes, you choose to survive! Also, keep in mind, you cannot be a child's friend, but at the same time, you must show yourself friendly! It is in the word, show yourself friendly so that your children will feel comfortable and confident when speaking with you. Children will come to a calm parent about anything they are facing right now! Parents, youth are killing themselves today from virtual bullying and we parents must pay attention! For example, my antenna went up, let me tell you why, a couple of weeks ago, my 13-year-old had an emotional response to classmates making fun of him because his microphone was not working properly during his virtual class period. As I observed him run, then fall on the floor, I realized how distressed he was, and

I told him to get up! Let us use our words together! My son shared what they were saying to him and that the teachers were not addressing to his satisfaction and it hurt him - he felt unprotected. I am grateful that I have an environment where all my children come to me instead of privately hurting on the inside, and using unhealthy coping mechanism such as cutting themselves, or going to their inexperienced friends receiving irrelevant advice, or even drinking or drug use. I am a longtime advocate of suicide prevention. Let me share this nugget with you before I go:

From my experience journaling has allowed me not only to express my thoughts and my feelings, but it has also helped me with my healing process. In 2013, I sat down with my family I gave them different notebooks, colored sticky notes, pens and presented an open platform within my own family. Today journaling is the very tool used to come closer together. With just a few times a week you can see a change. In March, observing the distress from COVID19, I decided that my family would revisit journalism as a unit, it has alleviated my younger children from running and just exploding. This has helped us from the daily pressures presented and the changes that life has presented today. With Journaling, not only does it release stress and a lot of tension from our shoulder, but it has also birthed great goals and is where dreams have become reality. Together our family problem solves and make great things happen! Journaling together has showed me clearly, I have learned that it is not as a parent yourself, what you say, it is how you say and present it! Try it for your family today!

MY GOAL IS TO TRANSPORT YOU TO A PLACE OF SUCCESSFUL PARENTING.

Sitting down talking to parents and youth about blessings and favor came natural for me! I did it effortless every day, all day. Teaching and educating our youth to be better and determine what they want to do in life as a child and work at it so they can do better than we did. I point out that they can even surpass the adults who they feel, may have failed them in life. Challenging youth to think, to want to strive for excellence and how to have something to show forth in life. If not a parent now, maybe later, what we do today, affects out tomorrow! Our parents tried to show us the things that we needed to do or talked about what they have done in their lives. They may have shared their failed attempts. There comes a time for a change in one's life to be better, to do better, to be more efficient and effective, to stand out and to be on top, to be a light in dark places! Everything we do, it matters! Everything we say it matters! From our words and experiences, we plant the seeds for our young ones. Are you cultivating your seed or are they bound by weeds? As Parents, what we do as our children's first, Leader can shape their future. It is our responsibility to help our new generation to reimagine life, it is not as we once knew it to be.

Be a straight shooter in love! Parents let's build up our children, despite past experiences! It is time to be more aware of lives changes, be alert, like the game of chess, we should have strategic intentions with everything that we do as great parents and it all does matter, to each one of us! Never forget to pay attention to our children, they will be the next leaders to follow in our footsteps! What paths are we paving for our youth? Parents lets stand up and stand out!

* * *

To learn more by enrolling in Juanita's masterclass, point your phone's camera at the QR code then click the link:

DR. JONAS
GADSON, DTM

Dr. Jonas Gadson, DTM, known as "Mr. Enthusiastic!" is an International Motivational Speaker, Trainer, Author, Radio Personality and Expert Communication Coach. He worked for two Fortune 500 companies, Xerox Corporation and Eastman Kodak Company. At Eastman Kodak Company he trained over 8,000 employees from 69 countries and achieved the Trainer of the Year Award. He brings 30 years of corporate knowledge, skills, expertise and experience to the speaking, training and coaching arenas.

In 2020, he was inducted into the Marquis Who's Who In America. He also spoke at the Wonder Women Tech Virtual Global Summit in London, England; the Black Speakers Network; and the Worldwide Multicultural Summit. He is a Distinguished Toastmaster, DTM, the highest level of achievement in this organization of 300,000 members worldwide. He has a Doctorate Degree in Theology and is also a graduate of Dale Carnegie. He was featured in Speakers Magazine, Pink Magazine and Beaufort Lifestyle Magazine to name a few! His Motto Is: "Since Greatness Is Possible Excellence Is Not Enough! Go For Greatness!"

CONTACT:

Partners For Purposeful Living LLC.

Email: jg@jonasbonus.com.

Get your FREE gift "How To Give A Powerful Presentation!" and learn more about how to Master Your Message!

Go to: *www.jonasbonus.com/freegift*

MAKE YOUR *Future* MATTER!

There are three kinds of people…Those who make things happen, those who watch things happen and those who wonder, "What happened?" I am a person who makes positive things happen and I believe that you are too! Bonus from Jonas, "Your future is so bright that you are going to need to wear sunglasses!" "Don't focus on what you have lost! Focus on what you have left! What you have left is enough to get the job done!" "You are next in line for a blessing! Don't get out of line. Don't detour. Don't let anyone cut in front of you! It's full steam ahead! Whatever you focus on the longest will become the strongest!"

This chapter will show you that you can face your future with a new focus! Because I have learned that "the best way to predict the future is to create it!" This is your time, and this is your turn! This is the decade for the doers! Congratulations on your wise decision to invest in the most important person on the planet, you! Bonus from Jonas, "A chapter a day keeps mediocrity away and welcomes greatness in to stay!" Welcome in greatness! In this chapter we are going to deal with the 3 V's, Vision, Value and Voice. **Vision** is how you see yourself. **Value** is how you feel about yourself. And **Voice** is how you think about yourself! I want you to know that you matter! To face your future with a new focus, we must make sure that your foundation is built on the 3 V's. Before I share with you the first V, allow me the privilege to share a little about me!

I am Dr. Jonas Gadson, DTM, known as "Mr. Enthusiastic!" an International Motivational Speaker, Trainer, Author, Radio Personality and Expert Communication Coach.

- I bring over 30 years of knowledge, skills, expertise and experience with two Fortune 500 companies: Xerox Corporation and Eastman Kodak Company in Rochester, NY. At Eastman Kodak I trained over 8,000 employees from 69 countries who were human resource professionals, managers, group leaders, engineers, salespeople, executive secretaries and manufacturing employees and I received the "Trainer of the Year" Award!
- When Dr. Gadson delivered a motivational message to the Professional Women's Engineering Group at Delphi Automotive, a manager came in and heard the last 10 minutes of his speech and was so impressed that she hired him on the spot! He met with her and did a needs assessment of her organization, custom-designed the materials and delivered a Two Dynamic Days at Delphi training for managers, supervisors, human resource professionals, union representatives, and manufacturing employees! As a result, he motivated them to increase their productivity and improve the company profitability!
- Dr. Dawna L. Jones, MD, a participant in Dr. Gadson's "How To Give A Powerful Presentation!" seminar in Boston said, "I felt empowered…confident to give my upcoming lecture…I am excited about what I was able to learn and can incorporate right away."

Now that I have shared a little about me, let's start with the first V:

Vision is what you can be; eyesight is what you can see. Some people have 20/20 eyesight but no vision. What do you see for your future?

BONUS FROM JONAS

"What you see is what you will be! And if you want to be more, you have to first see more!"

You must have a clear vision. My favorite book says that "without vision the people perish. But with vision, the people will flourish." When you realize who you are and whose you are, and the purpose you are here and the reason why you were given the gift, not only for yourself but to help others, you are eager to accomplish it!

Your vision will determine your future. It is where you see yourself. Where you are going and how you plan to get there. You understand that it is a process. My favorite book says, "Write the vision, make it plain then run with it!" I believe "If You Think it; Ink it!" Once your vision is written down and it is clear, run with it! You must take positive action to bring your vision to reality. "This is the Decade for the Doers!"

A young reporter looking to make a name for himself ran up to Ms. Helen Keller. He said to her, "Life must have been very difficult for you. Being blind and not able to see." Ms. Helen Keller answered him and said, "Worse than being blind is having sight but no vision." He had come from the perspective that being blind was merely a physical thing. Are you able to see your future? Or is someone or something blocking your view? What kind of future are you creating? As I said earlier, "the best way to predict your future is to create it!"

BONUS FROM JONAS

"When your vision is clear the results will appear!"

I have learned that you must be willing to work harder on yourself than you do on your job. I have learned that the biggest room in the whole wide world is room for improvement! You can always Better your Best!

In this decade, you must implement the two w's: work and worth. I like what the great orator Frederick Douglas said, "You might not get everything that you work for, but you must work for everything you get!" Whitney Young said, "It is better to be prepared for an opportunity and not have one, than to have an opportunity and not be prepared!" When we don't take the time to prepare, then we will spend our life in repair! This chapter is written to help you prepare for your future! And when you work on yourself and know that you are worth it, you will do the work!

BONUS FROM JONAS

"When your value is clear, your decision is easy!"

Value is at the core of the foundation that all of your principles, beliefs and integrity is built upon. It is non-negotiable! When you have value, your word is your bond, and your positive reputation precedes you. It is what you believe in strongly. "What you say and what others see is working together in harmony!" When you value yourself, you are building what is important to you. What you value defines you! It is your anchor, your foundational block, your guiding light, your compass. It is what helps you to navigate through the storms of life. You will not get lost if you have identified your true value. The four foundational blocks of value in my coaching business are Education, Inspiration, Transformation and Motivation!

I challenge you to define your value, because if you don't, you are doomed to follow someone else's. Your value is based on principles that guide your decisions. It is not only what you will not do, but also what you will do!

Your value drives the **3 C's: Conduct, Conversation and Character** in your life.

Conduct is, "What you say and what people see that is working together in harmony." It is your behavior. It is what you do and how you carry yourself.

Conversation: You want your conversation to be in alignment with your assignment! Because "life and death is in your tongue." What are you saying to yourself? Your subconscious mind believes your voice more than anybody else's. If you tell your subconscious mind what you can do, it will work to bring up all of your successes and what you have done that is positive. It is what you say to yourself about yourself, and your subconscious mind will work to make you right! You talk right and walk right! You speak positivity into your life and into the life of others. What I have learned is that if it is going to be, it's up to me! And if you are going to get through, it's up to you!

Character is who you are when you think that no one else is looking: It is the real you!

Mr. Cavett Roberts said that, "Character is the ability to carry out a good resolution long after the excitement of the moment has passed." However, it is a proven fact that most people make decisions based on their feelings, then they justify that decision with logic. What I have learned in life is that feelings make a wonderful passenger, but a lousy driver. Feelings are a reckless driver, seeking diligently a place to have an accident!

We have heard of weapons of mass destruction and we are fortunate that we do not have to deal with them in our everyday lives. But our challenge today is weapons of mass distraction! There are as many as 6,000 commercials that come on the television every day, along with your email, your texts, social media and the telephone. All of them are fighting for your undivided attention! They are taking you away from your dreams. Now, you aren't focusing on what you say you want! We must know exactly what we want when we go into a certain situation, and we will not come out with anything less. Being laser focused gives you the ability to achieve whatever your goal is, faster!

For example: When I go to the store to buy a navy blue suit, size 52 regular I am laser focused. I already know what I want. I go straight to the men's suit department, to the area where the size 52 regular suits are. I get the navy blue suit and try it on. If it fits, I grab it, buy it, bag it and I bring it home!

Here is another weapon of mass distraction and it can be deadly! Sometimes the darkest part of your life comes just before the dawn. We say, "there's light at the end of the tunnel." Investigate that light to make sure that it is not a train that is coming. Because you can be on the right track and still get run over! Don't be like the deer that gets distracted and becomes mesmerized by the headlights of an oncoming vehicle; it gets hit and loses its life! If the deer would look away from the light, and turn away from that distraction, it would realize that it can move out of the way and live!

When you are true to your value, you will not settle for anything less than the best!

Remember that you are fearfully and wonderfully made; you are special and biologically unique. What is your value? You owe it to yourself and to the world to honor your values and demonstrate your uniqueness; to be your best self on purpose.

When you identify and honor your worth to yourself; it is easy to identify and articulate your value to the world!

BONUS FROM JONAS

"You deserve to be heard!"

Voice. There are a lot of different voices; In the midst of all of these voices talking, we need to hear your voice! There are approximately eight billion people on the planet and there is no one just like you. No one else has your voice. No one has lived your story. Your story wasn't given to you just for you. It didn't just happen to you, it happened for you! We need to hear your voice. And the world needs to hear your story.

My Story Of Overcoming The Tumor In My Stomach! I was born in 1953 in Beaufort, SC at Beaufort Memorial Hospital; I was a healthy baby. And I was raised on St. Helena Island, SC on a plantation. But when I was a little boy of four years old, I became very sickly and my stomach was protruding out as if I were nine months pregnant! If you have seen the commercials on television with the starving Ethiopian children, you observed how their bodies were skinny, but their stomachs were big. This was how I was. My mother didn't know what was wrong. I was the sickest child out of all of my mother's children. But my mother was determined to find a cure for my health condition. She went to the midwives and they couldn't do anything! When we went to Beaufort Memorial Hospital, there was nothing that they could do either. I did not get better, I got worse! Then my mother rushed me to Roper Hospital in Charleston, SC. At the tender age of four, I had to undergo major surgery; my life was at stake! I had a tumor in my stomach that made it protrude out as if I were nine months pregnant. The doctors told my mother that they had operated on eight other babies who had the same condition I had, and all eight of the other babies died and that I was going to be number nine! I don't know if they had sterilized the utensils; maybe they were doing the operation to see what organs they could use for others. They operated on me not expecting me to live; they had the expectation that I was going to die anyway.

I remember coming out of surgery, heavily sedated and in pain, stitches all in my stomach. We thought that everything was alright after the surgery, but I got a massive infection! Before I could get over the first operation, I had to have a second operation immediately! When the doctors went back into my right side, to clean up the horrible infection, they realized that it had spread to my right kidney and they took that kidney out without telling my mother and without telling me. Therefore, I did not find out that I had only one kidney until fifty years later! I now had two operations, one on my stomach and the second on my right side near my ribs and my back! The two surgeries resulted in a very long journey on the road of recovery for me. I had gone into the hospital with a protruding stomach and came out with one kidney, and with two deep wounds and a limp that should have stayed with me for life. But it didn't! I am not just a survivor; I am an overcomer! The doctors had given me a diagnosis that I would die, but God gave me the final prognosis, that I would live!"

BONUS FROM JONAS

"Don't let anyone bury you until after you are dead.

You are bigger than that. You are better than that!
And the best is still in you! Allow that Best to bud,
to bloom and to blossom into a
bright and beautiful future!"

When I realized that as I shared my story it helped thousands of others, I began to say that it not only happened to me, but it happened for me! For me to give the gift of my story to others! Your story is not for you only; it is for you to overcome too and to tell others. Your story didn't come from you, it came through you! You must tell your own story, don't leave it up to someone else to tell it. You determine how your story starts and how it ends. Your story with you as the author can positively impact thousands of lives! I have learned that I must be a participant in my own rescue!

And to be an overcomer, so do you! Now, we need to hear your voice!

"If you are around the lame boy or lame girl, or the lame man or lame woman, you will learn how to limp!" Who is around you? And how are they affecting your voice? How is that affecting your talk? Your walk? How is that affecting your life? Are they affecting it in a positive way or in a negative way? How is that affecting your story? I say, "My whole life is a bonus!"

You must learn how to Master Your Message! Know yourself, know your subject and know your specific audience. As an Expert Communication Coach, I can help you tell your story positively, powerfully and purposefully! We need to hear your voice! Now when you tell your story, you demonstrate that you matter, and you design your own future; you face it with a new focus! Now, you are on your way to the top and cannot be stopped! The sky is not your limit; your belief is.

BONUS FROM JONAS

"If you cheat yourself in your preparation it will show up in your presentation."

As you incorporate these 3 V's into your life, **vision, value and voice** you demonstrate that you matter! Now you know that "the best way to predict your future is to create it!" **Bonus from Jonas**, "Read this chapter the first time for information! Then read it a second time to start your transformation!" Congratulations! On investing in the Most Important Person on the Planet, You!

Excerpt from my new book, *"How To Fly Like An Eagle With Wings Like A Wimp!"*

It teaches you how to *"Take A Chance! Take Charge! And Take Control of Your Life!"*

If you are interested in purchasing a specially autographed copy from me, the author, then call (585) 703-9547 to order.

"Since Greatness Is Possible
Excellence Is Not Enough!
Go For Greatness!"

* * *

To learn more by enrolling in Dr. Jonas' masterclass, point your cell phone's camera at the QR code then click the link:

KIMMOLY K. LABOO

Kimmoly K. LaBoo is a Bestselling Author, International Speaker and Certified Master Life Coach. She is at the helm of LaBoo Publishing Enterprise, as CEO and founder. She is a highly respected change agent in her community and around the world.

Her award-winning company was created for the independent self-publisher, to provide expert guidance and unlimited support, to help them recognize their brilliance by sharing their stories with the world as writers. She has an outstanding track record of producing bestselling authors through her publishing company and has written and published twelve titles of her own. With over 15 years writing experience, she shares her knowledge and lessons learned through speaking, writing and coaching.

Kimmoly believes, "We all have a story to tell, we just have to be willing to dig deep and find the courage to release it."

She was named among the Top 25 Women in Business by Courageous Woman magazine in 2018. She has appeared on Think Tech Hawaii, WPB Networks, Heaven 600 radio, ABC2News, FOX5 News, and has graced many stages speaking and training to include, Women World Leaders, Department of Veterans Affairs, Blacks in Government National Training Conference, and Coppin State University

CONTACT:

Website: www.laboopublishing.com

Email: staff@laboopublishing.com

FB/Instagram/LinkedIn: Kimmoly K LaBoo

Twitter/YouTube: @MsKimmoly

MAKE YOUR *Story* MATTER!

I believe it was Tony Robbins who said, "If you are going to go through pain in life you might as well get something out of it." Everyone I know has experienced some sort of pain or hardship in life. What matters most is how they got through it. We have some people who looked the storm in the face and dared it to take them out. We have others who let the pain of the events take them under or out. Some fail to realize that there is more healing in release than in isolation. Most will take their secrets to the grave trying to protect the people who've done them wrong. Many have buried the pain, failing to realize that it is still silently chipping away at their inner being.

Pause for a moment and think about it: What do you do with your pain?

I used to be the person who kept all of my feelings inside, not wanting to expose myself to those who'd hurt me. I often suffered in silence, with sadness buried deep beneath my smile and positive attitude. On the outside I was beaming; on the inside I was broken. But something happened in 2006. I was severely broken. I was on my second failed marriage and had returned to my first love, even though I knew our relationship was unhealthy. I went back to what was familiar, but again it ended with infidelity. I was now a single mom of two boys, financially and emotionally bankrupt, trying to figure out my next steps. I felt like I had lost everything. I was bitter, angry and full of un-forgiveness. Around the same time a new church opened in my community and I was invited to attend. For the next 12 years it would become my church home.

In my early days of being a member there, I spent a lot of time on the altar, and it seemed week after week the pastor always had something about forgiveness in the message. It honestly got on my nerves, but I know now that was because God was trying to get through to me. He wanted me to forgive so that he could continue to use my life. I struggled with this. I did not want to forgive and I was perfectly okay with being bitter, so I thought. God would not let up; he kept urging me to forgive, and then one day I heard so clearly in my spirit, *If you can't speak it, write it.*

That moment turned out to be a game-changer for me. I followed that instruction and it set me free. That was the beginning of my writing journey. I penned my first book in 2006. I wrote everything I was feeling. I poured years' worth of tears into chapters. I titled it *The Passion in My Soul.* I bared it all. It was in that writing process that things emerged that I didn't even know had taken root. I spared nothing and no one. It wasn't about them; it was about me—my healing. The funny thing is, I wrote it and thought, *That's it. I did it. I'm glad that's over.* Oh, how God must have chuckled. Writing has since become my shared therapy with the world. I have since penned 12 books, and I am still writing. My life is now an open book.

In my opinion, writing unlocks the mystery of who we really are. In fact, I challenge you as the reader of my words to begin to think about your life and the experiences you've encountered, endured, and perhaps overcome. Consider the notion that all you have been through wasn't about you at all. If that is the case, why hold on to it? For years I carried around baggage that didn't belong to me. When I started to unpack it, many opportunities opened up for me. Writing led to speaking, because when you know how to do something, people want to know how you did it. Speaking led to mentoring. Once I released my pain it was as if God showed me young women who had the same pain I once carried. Mentoring led to coaching. The work continued. I could see how God had carefully orchestrated everything. Writing, speaking, mentoring, and coaching led to traveling around the world sharing the many gifts and talents that were once six feet, ditch deep, within my being. I can assure you, I love the open book far more than the ditch, and pretty much predict that you will too.

Before my life became an open book I thought I was okay. However, looking back on it now, I know I was merely functioning in my dysfunction. Is that your story right now? Are you functioning in dysfunction? I've heard it said that you are only as sick as your deepest secret. Most people don't want to go back to the core of the issues that plague them, but that's where the gold is. You may wonder, how can that be? If you talk to any therapist the conversation usually begins with the statement, "So tell me about your childhood." That is because many of our issues stem from early trauma that we have hidden away in an attempt to move forward, not realizing that very thing that is tucked away can and will resurface at the most inopportune time. I would say before it sneaks up on you, go back and get it. Nothing in your life should be wasted, not even pain.

There is a great discovery and healing that comes with ripping the Band-Aid off old wounds. Although painful, it opens you up to a whole new realm of possibilities. Sharing your truth with others, becoming an open book, will give you newfound freedom of things you never imagined. For example, when my third marriage failed, I was embarrassed and devastated. I thought, *How could this possibly be my life?* Yet there I was, emotionally damaged and trying to figure out my next steps. My soul was tired; the verbal and emotional abuse I suffered in that relationship impacted me in ways I didn't recognize until I was outside the picture frame. It was horrible. However, from that whole ordeal a new book, ministry, and business was birthed. As I mentioned before, nothing in your life should be wasted. As a Christian woman I received criticism, limited support, and horrible advice, due to the negative stigma that is associated with divorce in the faith-based community.

In the midst of all of that trauma I was still speaking at women's conferences. At one of them, I had just finished speaking and there was a pastor there who invited people to come to the front of the room for prayer. The panel of speakers joined her in support. When she was done she turned to me. It was totally unexpected. She began to pray over me and she told me that it was not by accident that I had been through several failed marriages. She said God wanted to use me for a greater purpose. By the time she was done, I had cried off all of my makeup. Not long after that God gave me the vision for the Christian Divorce Coaching Center. I became a Christian divorce coach, supporting women of faith who were experiencing divorce and helping them to navigate the process and solidify their next steps. I created a safe place for them to fall and then rebuild. From that came my first anthology, titled *A Threefold Cord Broken - What Happens When Christian Marriages Fail.* It is a compilation of stories told by women in the faith- based community who have experienced divorce and are now thriving. What a beautiful way for God to bring the devastation of my failed marriages full circle. I have the compassion to assist, the knowledge to share, and the empathy needed to successfully guide women through painful transition to triumph.

Two years later, my amazing new life continued to blossom. I was presented with the opportunity to move to Honolulu, Hawaii. I had lived in Maryland all of my life. This would be a huge step for me. When I was going through the pain of walking away from what I thought was everything, my constant prayer was, "God please just give me peace; all I want is peace." Well, God far exceeded my expectations. He sent me to one of the most peaceful places in the world. There is where my true healing took place.

I never realized how noisy my life was until God literally sat me on an island. It was there that I discovered my true self. I was doing things I'd never done before. I looked in the mirror one day in amazement and asked, "Who are you?" I was taking long hikes through beautiful mountains, sitting on the beach for hours at a time, watching the sunset at the end of my days, riding along winding roads with no music on, just listening to the brushing sounds of the bushes, being shocked and surprised by beautiful rainbows, parasailing and attending luaus. My heart and my soul were healing. I could hear from God so clearly. He was giving me my true identity back. I was shedding every lie, hurtful word, and painful experience that no longer belonged to me, including my names of the past. It was there in Hawaii that I reclaimed my identity.

I hadn't had my birth name in over 20 years. God told me it was time for me to reclaim my name, so I did. I had no idea what was in store for me after that. Once my name change was completed and my family name was restored to me, God gave me the vision for LaBoo Publishing Enterprise, a publishing company that would allow me to assist others in crafting their stories to bring about healing in their own lives, thus impacting the lives of others. You see, I'd been doing it since 2006 when I wrote my first book anyway. Like I said, nothing in our lives is wasted if we are open to becoming an open book. I had all of the resources, I had built amazing relationships along the journey and now it was time to put my brand on it. It has been one of the most rewarding aspects of my life to date. I've met and published some of the most amazing people from all over the world. My business is thriving and I am in my zone, and guess what? It's all because I decided to allow my life to become an open book in order to serve others.

Can you imagine what your life would be like if you dared to let it be an open book? I know it's a scary thought. No one really wants to reach back and pull out their deepest secrets. However, when you think about how much of your life will go unlived if you miss this opportunity, I pray it will compel you to bravery. Nothing that we go through in life is for us; it is for us to be able to impact the lives of others. Don't waste your pain. Make your pain matter in a way that is undeniable. Someone is waiting for what you have to offer. They need to know how you survived whatever it is that you have been through. You may think, *Many people have already written about what I have been through;* however, there is a specific audience that is out there waiting just for you. They will respond to your voice in a way that they may not be able to hear from someone else. I'd dare say that it is selfish for us not to share our victories. You have been delivered through trial after trial and it is time for you to share how you made it through. There are doors waiting for you to burst through them.

Sharing the lessons that life has taught me has landed me in some pretty amazing places. One of the most extraordinary experiences I've had came as a result of a mentoring manual for teenage girls I created to support my mentoring organization. It afforded me the opportunity to travel to Ghana, West Africa, to speak at a Global Literacy Conference and to work in one of the villages training teachers on new and effective techniques to support their students. We were in classrooms without walls, with dirt floors, surrounded by beautiful children who were eager to learn and grateful for everything. I'd never seen anything like it. I was amazed.

On that trip I shared a room with a woman whom I only met when we arrived at the airport. There were 13 of us on the trip and we were also blessed to have famed poet Nikki Giovanni join us there as a part of the team. It was amazing. While we were on the small bus that carried us to the village, my roommate Caroline started talking about creating a children's book. We began to brainstorm and when we got to the village and saw the children, the vision became even clearer. We would take photographs of the children to include in the children's book. We planned a field trip for the day, venturing through the village. We asked the children to find items that corresponded with each letter of the alphabet. They had so much fun and we were equally as excited as we captured them in the moment.

When we arrived back in the States, we started the work of gathering the components needed to pull together our children's book. Our intention was to create the book and use it as a fundraising tool to support the children in the village. We also wanted to send the books back to the village so the children could see themselves in print. We did it! The children's book is titled *C is for Cocoa*. But you will never believe what happened next. Not long after the book was published we received a call from some movie producers who had somehow come across our book. They wanted to know if they could use our book in their movie. The movie was about child soldiers in Ghana, starring none other than Idris Elba! The movie was *Beasts of No Nation*. Perhaps you've seen it. If not, if you just happen to watch it someday on Netflix, it's within the first ten minutes of the movie. A mother is teaching her son his ABCs and they are reading from our children's book, *C is for Cocoa*. If anyone had told me that something I created would one day end up on a movie screen, I would have lost the bet. Writing has opened some incredible doors for me. Who knows what it will do for you. Can you just imagine?

I've shared multiple stories with you throughout this chapter because I want you to understand the impact that sharing your journey through the written word can have. Your stories matter; you just have to become brave enough to share them. Someone's healing, deliverance, joy, peace, and/or happiness may be tied to the release of your story. There is a great sense of accomplishment and fulfilment that comes from realizing the unforgettable impact you've had on the lives of others merely from sharing your story. Don't you dare leave this Earth with all of your untold stories buried inside you. Again, nothing in your life should be wasted. If you went through it, overcame it, survived it, and learned from it, teach it, speak it, and/or write about it.

One of the greatest gifts for me as the CEO of LaBoo Publishing Enterprise is journeying through the process with many amazing men and women, hearing them talk about what the process was like for them as they poured out their hearts onto the pages. They often share how much healing occurred during the process or things they discovered and learned about themselves as a result of writing. It is such a beautiful transformation. Then on the other side of it is the people who read the books that have been produced. It is absolutely unforgettable. I never tire of hearing the tremendous impact of the written word.

"There is no greater agony than bearing an untold story inside you."
~ Maya Angelou

Are you ready to write your story? Has this chapter sparked something in your soul? If so, I challenge you, over the next five days, to begin the process of telling your story. Create a list of every significant event, good or bad, that you have experienced in your life. Once you've completed your list take the next step and visit *www.laboopublishing.com* to schedule a consultation to discover how we can assist you in releasing the value behind your voice in the form of the written word.

Imagine the freedom you will feel when you are no longer bearing the weight of your untold story.

Don't wait. Create your list and visit: *www.laboopublishing.com* to schedule your consultation. We can't wait to work with you.

* * *

To learn more by enrolling in Kimmoly's masterclass, point your phone's camera at the QR code then click the link:

BRIAN J.
OLDS

Brian J. Olds wasn't born with a natural enthusiasm for public speaking.

A burgeoning change agent in the industry, the Baltimore native inadvertently entered the world of speaking when he delivered his first speech to the Morgan State University Toastmasters Club in 2006. Recalling this as one of his most defining life moments, Brian instantly connected to his passion when he found himself in front of a standing ovation at the conclusion of that speech.

Identified as a "curator of collaboration", Brian specializes in empowering rising professional speakers to create clarity, streamline systems, and cultivate the relationships needed to reach the unique audience they are called to serve. His passion for speaking, diversity and building relationships led him to create Black Speakers Network (BSN), a membership-based professional speaker development and empowerment company. With an active network of more than 10,000 speakers, BSN is committed to equipping, connecting, and inspiring the next generation of professional Black speakers.

With a deep appreciation for the artistry of speaking at the helm of his career, Brian J Olds is defining success on his own terms. His impact is illustrated perfectly in industry mate Zig Ziglar's quote, "It's not where you start – it's where you finish that counts."

CONTACT:

Social Media Properties:

Join Black Speakers Network FREE Facebook Community: *http://bit.ly/bsnfb*

Instagram Brian J. Olds: *@BrianJOlds*

Instagram Black Speakers Network: *@BlackSpeakersNetwork*

BSN Facebook Business Page: *https://www.facebook.com/BlackSpeakersNetwork/*

LinkedIn Brian J. Olds: *https://www.linkedin.com/in/brianjolds/*

Website Brian J. Olds: *http://www.BrianJOlds.com*

Website Black Speakers Network: *http://www.BlackSpeakersNetwork.com*

MAKE YOUR *Message* MATTER!

It was the same routine just a different day. The alarm clock goes off at 6:30AM. I hit the snooze button. 5 minutes later it was suddenly 7:30AM. I dash out of bed; quickly shower, shave, get dressed, grab a quick snack or coffee as I race out the door to my car.

There was a small window of traffic, a time bubble so to speak. If I left the house between 7:25 AM and 7:34 AM I could expect to make it to work by 8:00 AM. Leaving any time after 7:35 AM guaranteed that I was not going to arrive until 8:15 or later!

Morning after morning this was my reality. Sure, I could have physically got up earlier, but sometimes, I was so mentally exhausted that the signals transmitted from brain to my feet never made it. I was in a rut, every morning, for 11 years I drove into the same parking lot for my corporate job. As I made the walk from car into our building; I would look up in the sky and silently, ask myself, "how many more times am I going to do this? I rarely had a concrete answer for myself.

Don't get me wrong. I was very thankful to even have a job. I graduated from college in 2007. I was immediately hired after one interview. In 2008, when the bottom fell out of the economy, you can look to your left and look to your right and expect that one of you was going to be laid off, but I never was.

I was very thankful to be employed, but it is possible to be grateful and yet painfully unfulfilled at the same time. That is where I was in life and I imagine that is where you might be as you read this chapter. You know there is more to life than giving your most creative 40 to 60 hours a week to an employer when you could be building your own dream. If that is, you then I have some great news for you.

There has never been a better time in history to make the transition from full-time employee to full-time entrepreneurship. I am not just saying that to sound cool or to blow smoke at you. If you look at how far we have come with technology, flexible work structures, ability to leverage talent around the world and many other factors all add up to you leaving your job faster than ever...if that is your goal.

It was certainly mine. Some people valuable money to buy clothes, cars, the latest tech tools, big homes, or other material things. While all that is nice as the popular phrase at the time of this writing goes. It is the Freedom for me. In my opinion, financial freedom is the single most important resource you can have. That is, the ability to decide what you do, how you do it, when you do and who you do it with. As you can imagine, freedom is also, by logical extension, the most expensive thing you can buy as well. And the more money you make in a corporate job, the more money it will take to buy your freedom.

My goal for personal financial freedom was code named "Tuesday's at 10". This may sound silly at first and it is but hang with me for a moment. Unless you are taking a full week off, which I almost never did in my corporate career, most people will take a long weekend. Maybe you request off Thursday and Friday for a long weekend, or perhaps you take off Monday as well. But to me, Tuesday's were one of those days that people do not just 'take off' from work unless there is a great reason.

My goal was to be able to do whatever I wanted on any given Tuesday at 10AM in the morning. That could be sitting in Starbucks sipping a Grande white chocolate mocha latte with no whip (my go-to order), in no rush to go anywhere. It could be meeting up with a client or friend for brunch. It could also be a mid-morning run to Target with (FREE GAME) if you did not know, I am here to let you in on an entrepreneurship secret. Tuesday's at 10AM is the BEST time to go to Target in the entire week. You basically have the entire store to yourself and the customer to 'red shirt' ratio is about 1:10 – you will feel like a celebrity that where they shut the store down just for you.

Fast forward to today, I now have my Tuesday's at 10 and every other day of the week for that matter as well. My personal mantra every day is to Have Fun, Make Money, and Make an Impact. After 18 plus months of revenue growth and consistent income, I made the decision to leave my corporate job on Friday April 12, 2019. I drove off the parking lot at 5:38PM EST. I now wake up when I want, structure my week the way I like and do as much or as little work as necessary to meet my goals.

If this lifestyle sounds good to you, I can tell you there is nothing special about me. You can do the same and if you read and implement the information in this chapter you can most likely do it much faster than I did as well. To do this however, you must understand one fundamental truth about escaping your 9 to 5 that I did not even realize until I was driving off for the very last time. You see, I used to believe that I simply need to replace my income to leave my job, however it was deeper than that. What I discovered is that you do not need to replace your income as much as you need to replace the systems that currently generate your income. When you are working you get paid a specific amount of money in exchange for a specific amount of time you are working. That's your current system, and it is a powerful and reliable one at that. If you keep showing up and performing reasonably well, you will continue to get paid month after month.

To transition into full-time entrepreneurship, you need to replace your current income system with a new, but equally sustainable and predictable streams of revenue. To 'Make It Happen', it's not good enough to have a plan, you must also have a SYSTEM. Unfortunately, I see far too many aspiring entrepreneurs who are wasting their time and energy "grinding", instead of focusing on purposely building the one number one asset that will create a lifetime wealth: a community.

To support you with making this transition, I am excited to share the system I used as the primary source of revenue to facilitate my freedom journey. For the remainder of the chapter, I will be introducing you and walking your through my 3C's of Monetizing Your Message Through Community and Memberships

CURATE

INTENTIONALLY CRAFT THE VISION FOR YOUR COMMUNITY

Let us talk about the future of business. What do you think companies like Netflix, Amazon and Disney all have in common? On the surface, they may appear quite different. Netflix is the pioneer of streaming digital content whose name has become synonymous with lazy in-home dating. Amazon is the number one of the top 5 retailers in the U.S. and quickly becoming the default option for anyone looking to buy just about anything online in 3 clicks or less. And Disney, the easily the only adult in the room on this list having been founded in 1923 is the beloved entertainment and media brand that we all have grown up with. Despite these distinct market categories and service offerings, all three companies have figured and aggressively focused on one thing: if you want to stay in Business, you MUST create reoccurring revenue. And so, do you.

If you have never thought about creating a membership community this is the time to start. The reality is that whether you formalize a membership program or not, your customers will have a relationship with your company from the moment you engage with them. It is up to you to help shape what their consumer experience will be from the first interaction until their last. This is a thoughtful process that takes time, feedback, and constant adjustments to fine tune as you bring in more customers through into your ecosystem of products and services.

Customers who purchase from you once are much more likely to purchase from you again. If you can provide something that your customers want on a reoccurring basis then you have the foundation for a membership program. That "something" could be access to information, resources, discounts, exclusive experiences, a shared physical or digital resource, or even varying access to you directly. You can curate your membership program and community any way you want.

When I started Black Speakers Network's membership program in 2017, I literally surveyed our current email list. I shared my intention to start a membership, provided a list of basic elements I was planning to include and had them write in the price they would pay for the service. That is how we launched our initial membership program and set our pricing. The key here is to keep it simple and just grow along the way once you get started.

Big Money Tip #1: Write a vision, mission and values and standards for your community and share it on all your platforms. You want all you members to know what you stand for unapologetically so they can decide if it is the right place for them. You also need to unafraid to enforce your standards and eject people from your community who willfully violate your standards. If you don't, it only take a few bad members to destroy the culture you are creating.

CONNECT

ESTABLISH AND MAINTAIN MULTIPLE CHANNELS OF COMMUNICATION WITH YOUR TRIBE

At this juncture, let's take a step back and establish some broad definitions for the purpose of this chapter. This will help you think more deeply about what you are creating and how your members will engage you. Here are my own definitions for the following terms:

Subscription – A subscription is a regular and reoccurring financial transaction that takes place when you enroll in a program. It is possible to have subscribers who are paying monthly or annual fee but still not have a community. Netflix for example has millions of subscribers but they do not really offer much in the way of community.

Membership – Membership is the actual program that your members experience and receive upon enrolling. When you create membership, you are agreeing to provide your customers real and consistent value over a fixed period. In exchange, members are also agreeing to uphold certain standards and values as a condition of their membership. It is possible to have members without subscribers and to have members without an established community.

Community – A community is the physical or digital environment where members can engage with the organization or each other. You can have various communities divided by level of access, areas of expertise or any other factor. How members feel when they experience your community will directly impact their decision to subscribe and if they want to continue to be members. Your members need to feel included, safe, and valued.

Establishing regular communication with your members is critical and one of the best ways to do that is to create a shared community. In Black Speakers Network we use many channels to stay in regular and consistent communication with our community as well as our paid members. This includes email, live or virtual events, text message, and social media groups. Your members need to keep you top of mind and hear from you consistently. This does not mean you need to spam, annoy, or bombard them with information but rather, you need to create a consistent presence in their life.

Most importantly, you need to invite the opportunity for two-way dialogue with your tribe so you can capture valuable feedback and improve your membership experience as you grow. Silent members tend who do not engage in your community, respond to emails, text or even calls tend to be the first ones to fade away so be sure you have a process to monitor ant track engagement.

Big Money Tip #2: Create a monthly calendar of how you will engage with your community and the type of content you will share. This can be a mix of articles, videos, live presentations, surveys, fun challenges or other activities that will keep members energized and eager to learn more.

CONVERT

CREATE CONSISTENT OPPORTUNITIES TO WORK WITH YOU ON A DEEPER LEVEL

From the very first moment one of your members hears about you and your organization the relationship process has started. Your role is to move the right people down the path of their customer journey to becoming a paid member. Depending on what you are selling this may happen immediately or may take serval weeks or months for people to decide that you have what they need. As a you are building your membership community the overwhelming focus should remain on creating value for them and showing that you care about their individual success.

If you are promoting and selling every time your members hear from you, they will eventually just tune you out as noise.

You members need to know that you are knowledgeable, trustworthy, and consistent. People appreciate feeling like they can connect with a real person who cares about their situation. Never forget, there is a real person on the other side of every transaction. No matter how big your community may become, never forget that people are not numbers they are people. They have goals, dreams, fears, desire and all the other emotions that we all face. When you offer value first and extend people and invitation to work with you. For your ideal customers, it then because the natural next logical step to work with you at a deeper level.

Big Money Tip #3: In most email marketing tools, you can track the engagement rate of your members to see who is getting closer to wanting to buy from you. Be sure to pay attention to open rates of your emails, click through rates to determine how effective your offers are. Take note of the things like the time of day and the type of content that your tribe respond best to so you can model past success. Be sure to remove members who never open your email, so they don't hurt your overall list. If a person does not open any of our emails after 90 days we drop them from our email.

CONCLUSION

You can do it! I know you can. There are people out there waiting for you to move out of your own way and create the community they need to grow to the next level. I believe in you! Do not let the desire for perfection stand in the way of progress. At this point in your life and career, you like have enough knowledge and expertise to serve thousands, if not, millions of people. If you are not happy with where you are in life, the good news is that only you can change it. However, the bad news is, only you can change it.

Building a community and a membership network is not always the fastest or easiest but, in my experience, it is the most sustainable way grow long-term repeatable income. It does not mean you need to only rely on memberships revenue, but the consistency of knowing you do not have to start every month back at zero is one of the best feelings an entrepreneur can experience. I want that for you, but you must want it more for yourself. If you made it to the end of this chapter and found this information helpful, I invite you to shoot me an email right now to *BrianJOlds@BlackSpeakersNetwork.com* with the subject line Make It Matter and let me know how you will leverage the 4C's to grow your business.

As we say in Black Speakers Network Speak Up! Your Audience Awaits...

* * *

To learn more by enrolling in Brian's masterclass, point your phone's camera at the QR code then click the link:

SUZANNE PETERS

"You can create the life we want", words Suzanne Peters stands by whole heatedly, after proving it with her own life. Suzanne uses her experiences and lessons learned from her own life transformation, to empower women and audiences worldwide to get clear on what they want and make it their reality.

Suzanne Peters is a law of attraction and business coach. She is the founder of Woman To Woman Empowerment and Social Network LLC, a company whose goal is to empower women worldwide, to live life on their terms and be an inspiration to others, via events, workshops, transformational speaking and books. Suzanne is the author of the book Woman To Woman – How To Create The Life You Want and the host of the Woman To Woman Conversations Podcast and YouTube channel, where she invites women from around the world to share their advice, tips and strategies to inspire others.

Suzanne is also the CEO and Founder of Woman To Woman International Network Inc. a 501 C (3) non-profit organization that supports the personal and business development of women through grants.

CONTACT:

Website: suzannepetersllc.com

Website: womantowomannetwork.com

Social Media: @suzannepetersllc

Social Media: @thewomantowomannetwork

MAKE YOUR *Pain* MATTER!

Just before breaking point, a bow holds an immense amount of potential energy - the most it can hold. The greater the tension, the greater the potential. It is one of the many beautiful conundrums that fall just shy of the paradox category. As you draw it back further and further you place it under more and more pressure, until every part of it exudes tension.

I reached that point just over three years ago - I was broke, depressed, lonely and just so tired. You see, I began my adult journey married to a controlling and abusive man with a lot of pride. His blows were unexpected but subtle. He was careful not to go too far. Always making sure I looked picture-perfect on the outside. They say a picture is worth a thousand words but in my case, it hid them - each one more heart-breaking than the next. He only bruised me where they could not be seen. I mean, God forbid if anyone were to find him out. His real weapon… was his words. My rock-solid self-esteem was worn down to sand. My pride, confidence, identity. I was his little puppet with barbed wire for strings. He convinced me he was there for me. He convinced me I would never find a man as good as him and I believed every word.

It took everything in me to find the strength to leave him. I looked for solace in another man only to find myself falling in the arms of a selfish lover. Someone who took advantage of me, every way he could before we parted ways. He did not like me, he just liked what he could get my desperate self to do for him. He at least gave me a parting gift… a sexually transmitted infection. Not a conventional present but one that seems to be increasingly popular.

I felt like a voyeur watching dominoes fall, but each domino was another part of my life and at times a part of me. Falling. One after the next. With nothing to stand on and worse still, nothing to stand for.

As if life was now toying with me, my business failed. It didn't just fail. It completely collapsed, irrecoverable. Nothing left to show but debt and paperwork. All my blood, sweat, and tears - gone in an instant. I lost everything and inherited a mountain of debt. The question of "why me?" followed like a shadow. Following me through the day, engulfing me at night. It was a question I kept asking for a long time. I felt stuck, confused, and embarrassed. The only thing I had left to show for myself was my work but even that was taken away. There seemed to be nothing I could take pride in. Nothing to look back on nor anything to look forward to either. I was caught between a hellish past and a hopeless future - lost in a perpetual battle with the present.

I confided in a friend, who had troubles of her own. She suggested we go into business together as a way of solving both our problems. Imagine my surprise when my business partner ran away with the business we built together. A few months before that happened, I called her my friend, and she had the audacity to say the same.

I lost faith in love, friendship, and worst of all, myself. Every day felt like I was living inside a deflating balloon, claustrophobia slowly replacing the breathable air. I do not think I can even begin to describe the level of despair. I was always optimistic about life. But for the first time, I reached such a level of unhappiness that I began to wonder if happiness was genetic. Like blue eyes, you were either born with it or you weren't. If misery was a song, my life was the melody.

I was on the threshold of the break point. Living in a tension that threatened to tear me apart - my metaphorical bow seemed destined to snap. But in that tense state, there are two things that could happen. Either the bow will be held in that tension perpetually and eventually warp until that shape becomes normalised, or the string will be released.

The sad reality is that a lot of people settle for the former - for a while I did. They stay stuck with the same pain and unhealthy habits for years. They become numb to the anguish. Disfigured. Being distorted is a temporary pressure but being disfigured is a permanent position. I sat on the verge of disfigurement for quite some time, in fact, I was almost there. The thing about disfigurement is that it is only completed in death. You may be going through a disfiguring time, but you are only truly disfigured when you die having never made a change. At a fundamental level, failure is not doing anything. If you do a bad job you don't fail. School might try to convince you that if you don't get a certain mark then you fail. The truth is that all it takes to overcome failure is to do something. If you do it badly you did not fail, you learnt. You narrowed the pathway to truth, success, love - or whatever else it may have been that you were pursuing. A pivot is all it takes to overcome failure, to break the mould of disfigurement. Though bear in mind that a pivot doesn't change where you are, just where you are facing. It is a decision to change direction. The distance comes later.

Speaking of distance, you obviously can't get any if you don't have an arrow. This may seem evident in the analogy, but it is significantly less obvious in the situation of which it is analogous. If you know anything about bows you will know that you should never shoot it without first notching an arrow. It's what they call dry firing. And the reason why you shouldn't do it is that all the tension and energy stored up in the bow has no release and ends up destroying itself. The string concentrates most of the tension but without an arrow, it just reverberates back into the bow and snaps it - in the real world, we call it suicide.

Having a channel to release both tension and energy is often something we are not acutely aware of - I know I certainly was not. The night I hit the pinnacle of my despair I ravaged the house for pills I could overdose on. When I couldn't find any, I picked up a bottle of bleach and challenged it to a battle of wills. With the bottle so close to my lips I wanted so bad to have my last toxic kiss. I couldn't. I couldn't even do that right. It was the ultimate shame. I was not even capable of erasing my seemingly worthless self.

But what would happen if you took an arrow from the quiver and notched it to the string? This is the choice I want everyone to make - to notch an arrow. It is the road that lies at every crossroad. If you were to load an arrow into the bow, it suddenly becomes useful, a tool for change. A weapon. I think it is high time we weaponised ourselves. Not as instruments of destruction but rather taking a stand against ignorance, apathy, anxiety, and depression. Declaring war on stagnancy, insecurity, inferiority complexes and more. They called World War One "The Great War", but the battlefield of the mind truly is. Notching in an arrow is that pivot, it doesn't change your environment at first, only your attitude towards it. But as you start to take aim and release, you begin to shape it. You release that tension and discover a newfound power. We think tension is a bad thing, but it's just stored energy and with the right release that pressure we felt becomes leverage.

Instead of drinking bleach, I decided to pour out the toxicity that I had been bottling up. I needed the strength to purge my mind. I couldn't do it without some kind of help. I needed to find that leverage. My unsaid prayer was answered from the most unlikely of places. I had been playing really depressing music online when unexpectedly the next video to come on was a Les Brown speech. As I tried to will myself to reach over and skip the video so I could go back to listening to music, the interview Oprah did with the author of "The Secret" came on. This caught my attention.

I listened intently as they spoke about The Law of Attraction and I soon realized this could be the answer I was looking for. I wanted to know more and that night dove head-first into a world that until then was unknown to me. More accurately, I dove into a methodology that taught me how to create my own world - a world that I wanted. Not one that I was better off without me, but I world that I made better. A world that I dreamed, defined, declared, and developed. That was the kind of empowerment the Law of Attraction gave me.

So, what is it?

The Law of Attraction, in the simplest terms, is the belief that positive or negative thoughts bring positive or negative experiences and things into a person's life." The belief is based on the idea that people and their thoughts are made from "pure energy", and that a process of 'like energy' attracting 'like energy' exists, through which a person can improve their health, wealth, and personal relationships.

I first had to come to terms with the fact that like gravity, the law was real. I couldn't see it or feel it, but it was there and it's always working. Whether I acknowledged it or not and whether

I believed it or not. Ignorance is not bliss when it comes to the Law of Attraction. Imagine having no understanding of gravity at all. If your frame of reference for existence was a fish, you might assume that you could move around in air the same way a fish does in water. This would lead to all sorts of issues - some amusing, like jumping up and expecting to keep going up; and some less amusing, like stepping off cliffs thinking you could keep walking. These kinds of situations are comical... until you realise that is what you are doing by ignoring the Law of Attraction - you are causing unnecessary discomfort, at best you will not reach your full potential, but at worst you will be sitting on your kitchen floor with a bottle of bleach in your hand and an emptiness in your heart. I was at that extreme, which is why I am so passionate about making people aware of what this can do for them.

I'm not saying it will be easy, growing up in a Christian household made learning about this pretty complicated and at times difficult to accept. But I decided for this power to be possible, it had to be from God. It had to be God's way of showing us that with faith, anything is possible. Thankfully, the Bible has the basic principles in it - like being "transformed by the renewing of your mind". The Law of Attraction, I decided, was a gift from God, and it was one I would use to create the life I always wanted. Then I would go out and teach others.

Now we can sit here and argue the science of it all day, but I didn't come here with a hypothesis, I came here with a story. My story. People can and do call it pseudoscience. But that doesn't change what happened to my life when I applied the mentality. I projected an incredible future in my mind and then watched the movie play out in real life. I went from a hellish life to a magnificent one. I am now happily married to a man I am convinced was created just for me. I possess my own beautiful house, with a closet the same size as my old bedroom - it sounds unbelievable, but it's true. I am now building my dream business, teaching others to create the life they want and love.

I travel and literally live life on my terms every single day. I could not be happier. The most amazing part to me is that all of this change, everything I achieved, I did it all in one year.

You see, I chose to believe that my vision of the perfect life was possible and most importantly, I was willing to go all in. I became obsessed. I lived and breathed the Law of Attraction and applied it to every area of my life. I chose to believe there was more for me in life and I wanted it all. This created what I would call a shift in my mindset and that's when I realized I have infinite potential. I had it all along but didn't quite see it until then, because it was dependent on how I chose to look at my life every day. I am utterly convinced that there is a level of potential inside of you that you are not even aware of. Neuroplasticity is a term that speaks of your brain's ability to change. Your thoughts and words shape the way your mind thinks, which in turn impacts the way you approach things - it can be a vicious cycle or one of compounding benefits.

Consider the difference between a winner and a loser. This is the law of attraction right in action! A winner manages a small win at some point and that leads to bigger and bigger wins each time. However, a loser attracts a loss at some point and that failure becomes bigger and bigger with every step. I chose to be a winner. To learn from my losses and let that be the end of it. To make the first win the battle of my mind, to reshape my perspective.

This alone couldn't create the change I was seeking, but it helped me to develop a special set of skills that allowed me to realize what I genuinely wanted and keep going for it, no matter what came my way. In today's world, it is easier than ever to lose focus and difficult to stay motivated. We live in a time dominated by consumerism; everything is trying to grab your attention and make you pay for it. If your focus is not on yourself enough, you will always be paying, but if it is on yourself, you will be investing.

Selfishness is not even part of the conversation we are having so don't get confused. Giving your time to develop and improve yourself is not selfish - it is necessary. Focus is a great start but having the right tools to both guide and remind me of the bigger picture, when I wasn't feeling up to it, helped change the game.

I don't mind sounding like a broken gramophone if it means people step out of their brokenness. The power of the mind is incredible, and the Law of Attraction capitalises on that fact. George Orwell said, "reality exists only in the human mind and nowhere else". There is a sutra that says that "reality exists where we create a focus". I don't necessarily agree with everything all the people and philosophies that hold this same belief say, but the fact that from Biblical principles to atheism you will find a lot of support for the power of the mind lends it some credibility. Enough to put some faith in it, or at very least to try it out. Its track record of success is of a magnitude like no other.

It's time to dream your future, feel it, believe it, and act as if it were - you will soon see it come to pass. By that, I don't mean spend a million dollars credit, I just mean that your attitude towards life, opportunity, and success - will shape the outcome of those very things.

Remember, the stretch is not the end. It is only a part of the process to achieve something more. I had many years of stretching, nearly to the point of breaking. But in just one year of consistently notching an arrow - I have completely turned every area of my life around.

A guitarist doesn't strive to hold back the string, their goal is to pick or strum. Likewise, the archer only draws when they have both an arrow and a target. Load an arrow, pick your target, and like the ancient archers of old, imagine yourself shooting and hitting the bull's eye over and over again. Feel the rush. Watch the next arrow split the previous one in half as it hits dead centre. The Law of Attraction holds a realm of possibility you never even imagined - which is exactly the point.

Weaponize yourself.

It's time to shoot your shot.

* * *

To learn more by enrolling in Suzanne's masterclass, point your phone's camera at the QR code then click the link:

MIKE POWELL

Mike Powell, MBA is a leadership consultant and business coach who, ignites passion, growth and energy for positive change in people and organizations in every sector. A dynamic speaker and trainer, Mike draws upon the lessons learned from his unique life experiences to help individuals, teams and organizations improve their performance and achieve success. With over 20 years of experience Mike has delivered keynote speeches, facilitated engaging workshops and led large scale consulting initiatives for organizations across the country. Through his inspiring message audiences across the globe have been inspired to reach their goals.

As Vice President of the Powell Consulting Group, a management consulting firm in Hyattsville, MD. Mike has worked with leaders in some of the nation's leading organizations and federal agencies including Johnson & Johnson, The Department of Homeland Security, the Environmental Protection Agency, The National Education Association, the Department of Housing and Urban Development, and the United States Department of Agriculture.

He is the co-founder of The Lifting As We Climb a 501 C (3) non-profit organization that supports the development of youth in communities across the country.

CONTACT:

Email: *mike.powell@mpconsultsondemand.com*

Web: *www.mpconsults.com*

Instagram/Twitter: *@mpconsults*

MAKE YOUR *Goals* MATTER!

On July 1, 2020, Ryan C. Greene and Mike Powell sat down for an interview about setting goals and overcoming the negativity that was 2020. Mike discussed how setting goals has positively impacted his productivity and profitability, as well as shared three key points of focus for setting life changing goals. This chapter features an excerpt of that conversation.

RYAN C GREENE: Mike, thank you so much for sitting down with me to day to share your insight on goal setting. I love how you teach a topic that's been around forever in the personal development space and totally flip it to make it relevant and innovative. How did this become your area of mastery?

MIKE POWELL: This goal setting teaching I created really started as a result of something we did years ago. We used to do the Dream Day events you created for middle and high school students. Something really hit me during that time. I realized we were starting early with these young people on setting goals. That was something that I didn't really talk a lot about when I was a young person. So, it just kind of struck me at that time as something that was important. And I just have continued to refine my process and refine my method and really take it to a new level every single year. Now I use my GoalDiggerAlerts™ method in trainings, coaching, and workshops all across the country.

RYAN: Awesome. So, what are the keys to effective goal setting, especially during these times?

MIKE: When it comes to goal setting, what I do is really focus on three things. I want us to think about how we can be RESILIENT during this time. I want to think about how we can be REFLECTIVE. Then I want us to walk away feeling RE-ENERGIZED.

Let's start with talking about being resilient. I teach emotional intelligence. A lot of people are familiar with the term emotional intelligence. They may think about emotional intelligence as how we interact with other people. How we engage with them. How we demonstrate empathy. How we hear them. How do listen to them. But a big piece of emotional intelligence is how we take care of ourselves. And that's where resilience comes in.

How are you able to bounce back from setbacks? How are you able to bounce back from stress? How are you able to deal with change and deal with the unexpected? And right now, after the year 2020 and beyond, all we've been dealing with is change and unexpectedness. Things went very differently than the way we planned them or the way that we saw them in our mind. Being resilient gives us the opportunity to say, "You know what? I can deal with this."

RYAN: As tough as things have been, what are the secrets to building that resiliency?

MIKE: Think back on those moments in your life when you had to bounce back. I remember being in high school and having hoop dreams and tearing up my knee. I realized basketball was not going to be my thing. I remember getting fired from a job. I remember not getting promoted. I remember not hitting my sales goals. I remember my first marriage failing. And I remember all those things and feeling like the world was going to end. Yet I'm still here. I'm still thriving. I'm still surviving. And when I look back, I see how those moments helped me to become stronger. Those are moments that helped me become the person that I am today. Those are moments that brought me here in this space and having this conversation with you even right now. Being a resilient person and being able to look back over my life and look at those experiences and obstacles that I've overcome gives me confidence.

Take some time to really think about how resilient you have been over your lifetime. All the setbacks, yet you are still here. You are reading this book, participating in the online masterclass, evaluating your goals, thinking about how to move forward, because you have been resilient. So, don't beat yourself up. Don't get down on yourself. Don't kick yourself because things haven't gone the way they planned. Instead, figure out how you can use these moments to build character, to build strength, and to become the person that's even stronger coming out of all we experienced the past few years.

RYAN: This is powerful stuff, Mike. Let's talk about being reflective.

MIKE: In my goal setting process and in our workshops, one thing that I really force people to do; it's not even something I encourage, I literally force people to do it, is to write down their goals. I want you to write down your goals, because I want you to be able to go back and have something to look at and remember when you said, "These goals were important to me at that time. This was a goal I had set for myself. This was a vision that I have for myself, this is where I wanted to be." It's important to go back and reflect on those things, because maybe those things aren't important anymore. Maybe there were some things that you just wrote down because it sounded good.

I remember a few years ago I was doing one of my workshops and I identified a goal for myself. I said I wanted to start a podcast. It seemed like everybody was starting podcasts. So I said, "Hey, I'm a speaker. I can start a podcast. This is what I'm going to do." I set my goals and I had plans and put everything in motion. Then I asked, "Why am I going to start a podcast? I know too many people that have podcasts. If I want to speak, I can just call Ryan and get on his show. I can call Felicia and get on her. There's no need for me to spin my wheels and put in the effort and do the things that people that I'm already connected to and have relationships with have already perfected." Even though that was a goal of mine when I wrote it down, when I went back to really look at it, to really reflect on it, I realized that wasn't really important to me.

The other side of that coin is that we also have some goals that were important to us, yet we simply didn't take the time to put in the effort and work to make it a reality. Reflect on those missed opportunities. Every year at my workshop, people talk about starting new businesses. They say they're going to get incorporated. They're going to form their LLC. I guarantee you that many of those people who said that in January 2020 did not do that. Failing to complete that goal ended up being a bigger missed opportunity because they missed out on any government money given out to registered businesses because of COVID.

RYAN: True indeed. Mike, this is good stuff. So after resilient and reflective, what's the final step?

MIKE: So, I want you to be resilient. I want you to be reflective. Then the last thing I want you to do is get re-energized. Right now, many people have lost their fire. It's not burning as bright. Life has some of us to the point where we are almost stuck. We're sad. We're hurt. We're emotional, we're frustrated, we're angry. We're working from home or we're doing family and we have kids, and all these things are happening all at the same time. You may be feeling overwhelmed, but now is the time for you to remember why those things are important to you. What is your purpose?

I have a one-year-old daughter. One of the silver lining of this pandemic has been that I've been able to be home with her every single day for her entire life. With my business, I travel frequently. With all my business, all of my training, all my workshops, all of my coaching, everything going virtual, I've been home with her every single day. That's really been important and exciting and good to be able to watch her grow. What it has really done for me is solidified what my purpose is. My purpose is to start creating opportunities for her, start creating resources for her, start creating an environment where she can grow and thrive and be successful.

I give her the best opportunities to be successful in life. Because of that, I'm re-energized. I've reignited my flame because now I have this little girl looking at me every single day asking, "What are you going to do? Where are we doing today? I don't care about who you talked to. I don't care how many followers you have. I don't care about you presenting at that conference, I am ready to play. Are we going to play or what?" So, with all the things that I've done in my life, all the money, and the cars, and the vacations, and all those things that I thought were just so important to me, I've been able to get re-energized about my purpose because my daughter is my purpose is right now.

I encourage you to rediscover your purpose to re-ignite yourself. Re-ignite that flame that burns on the inside. Remember your purpose. Remember why you got started. Remember why you get up and go to work. Remember why you deal with all the crap, the drama, and the people. Remember what you're doing it all for. If you can get in touch with that and reignite your purpose, then you will be well on your way to making your goals matter and putting yourself in position to achieve your goals and make your dreams come true.

RYAN: Mike, that was such a powerful teaching. So many valuable lessons were packed into this conversation. How can people get more information and work with you?

MIKE: Ryan, thank you so much for having me. It's always a pleasure to serve your audience. For those who want to further the conversation and get to work on setting their goals, please email me at mike.powell@pcgconsults.com or by visiting www.mpconsults.com. They can also follow me on Instagram and Twitter at @mpconsults.

* * *

To learn more by enrolling in Mike's masterclass, point your cell phone's camera at the QR code then click the link:

JACQUELINE
SHAULIS

Whether a group of Fortune 100 executives or at-risk teens, "The Excitable Introvert" Jacqueline Shaulis imbues her work with empathy, empowerment, engagement, and excellence to get people thinking, talking, and taking action that shifts their world for the better as they embrace their *AWESOME*.

From a challenging upbringing of abuse and self-harm, Jacqueline leveraged her successes, failures, quirks, and proficiencies to become an international speaker in nearly 20 countries and three-time international bestselling author, whose work has been translated into 7 languages. She brings fresh, unique perspective gained from her background as an award-winning performer, past newspaper columnist, broadcast journalist, and college instructor (all by voting age!).

Known for her *"energy, enthusiasm, and flair"*, Jacqueline invites her fellow introverts to embrace their *AWESOME* by sharing their Amazing Works of Expression Serving Others with Maximum Enjoyment, as they engage their gifts and empower their world. Through practical strategies, entertaining stories, and a dash of woo, she gives audiences the tools and confidence to co-create a life in word, thought, and deed that makes their hearts rejoice and causes a ripple effect of positive change in their world of influence and impact.

She is the founder and CEO of Awesome Enterprises LLC, creator of the *Mistress of Her Domain* series and podcast, best-selling author of nearly two dozen books whose work has been translated into 7 languages, and proud mom and aunt of 9.

CONTACT:

Website: http://iEmbraceAwesome.com

All social media: *@JKShaulis*

MAKE YOUR *Awesome* MATTER!

BECOMING AN INFLUENTIAL INTROVERT BY SHARING YOUR AMAZING WORKS OF EXPRESSION SERVING OTHERS WITH MAXIMUM ENJOYMENT.

What do you do with conflicting conviction?

Imagine yourself joyously exploring the facets of the human condition over a nosh with a dear friend. Or feeling the enthralling rush of diving into loving service to help a client solve her most stubborn frustration.

Now, imagine a feeling of deep, abiding aversion creeping over you as you attempt networking...small talk...selling.

You see, this was my dilemma. I love people but hate peopling. My heart longs to serve, yet the process of engagement leaves much to be desired. It's like cooking a stellar dish that would make even Gordon Ramsay smile - then having to do the dishes. Just the thought of it makes me want to Homer Simpson into the nearest shrubbery and politely disappear.

Around 2008, my quiet, "perfect on paper" life was being thrown into upheaval by an internal call for something bigger. My dissatisfaction with my life, and my subsequent guilt about feeling dissatisfied, pulled me away from everything I trusted as secure and launched me into orbit, untethered.

Professional speaking and training beckoned me to use myself and my story as a guide for other professional women on a journey to embrace their AWESOME by sharing their Amazing Works of Expression to Serve Others with Maximum Enjoyment.

So, what do you do when your happy place is being left the bump alone, yet you are being pulled into a greatness that requires spotlight, presence, and people? My answer didn't come by epiphany (although, maybe a little). What I discovered is that when we introverts direct our inward energy outward with laser focus, we can change the world through our presence.

Seeing Yourself Truthfully

The influential know that in order to conquer the competition, they must play to their own strengths and mitigate their own weaknesses. When you are willing to truthfully look at all aspects of yourself - not just the "good" or just the "bad" - you are best equipped to handle any inevitable challenge and every undeniable success. Each peak and valley of your experiences give you the lessons, tools, and insights to outrun, out maneuver, and outperform the competition.

My journey started ages ago in high school. I was always the quiet girl with a book sitting on the side or in a corner somewhere making smart aleck comments to anyone in my under-my-breath vicinity. I had a handful of friends but didn't really chat much with anyone.

Well, one day, I decided I'd had enough of that noise. I thought, "if I were the ideal version of myself, not the quiet wallflower but the me in my mind, who would that be? What would that even look like?" And so, I began to reevaluate what it meant to be an introvert.

Introverts are not just people who are quiet, or who are shy. They're not just reserved, or private, although any of those things can be true. An introvert is someone who gets their energy and motivation by having quiet reflection within themselves.

We introverts tend to create our own worlds, have our own conversations, ruminate entire successes or failures, all in our mind. We are our own best friend or worst enemy, depending on the day, and find it quite a task to engage with others because it depletes our energy mentally, physically, and emotionally.

It's from our inner world that we are able to create and shape and live - or dodge living as I was doing. It took me truthfully looking at myself to realize I was using my introverted nature to justify dimming my light. It wasn't that I didn't want to be in the spotlight - I just didn't want to have to deal with people all the time.

And so, I made the decision to show up more fully, that I would say yes to opportunities, and I would look for outlets for my ideas and creativity and passions. That space of truthful, decisive action is where the magic began to unfold.

It put me on a path that led to every good and perfect gift in my life. It began with me joining the debate team, which led me to transferring to a school where I thrived as a performer and teenaged college instructor. It introduced me to the competitive speaking circuit, which helped me pay for college and led to meeting the man who would become my husband and the father of my future son. It put me on a path of traveling the globe, becoming an international professional speaker, and publishing nearly 20 books (including three #1

Amazon best sellers globally). It created space for me to guide women on five continents to "Embrace Your AWESOME" in ways that honor them and those they impact at work, home, and beyond.

All of it started with me seeing myself truthfully.

FOOD FOR THOUGHT

I challenge you to take a moment to think of your best self, your highest self:

- What decisions and actions would you need to take that would allow that version of you to show up?
- What single action can you take in your business in the next 24 hours to show up as a champion?

Are you aware of the truth of yourself? Or are you allowing your influence upon your highest self to be diminished because you think that, as an introvert, you can't BE "those things"?

Honor Yourself Through Service and Love

Now you may think that once a lesson is learned, that's it. But if you've lived even a little bit, you know that's not always the case. The two-edged sword of this pandemic and post-pandemic life for us introverts is that although we don't have to navigate people nearly as much as before, there also are no pre-designated outlets to encourage, nudge, or cattle-prod us into coming forward and pursuing those crucial social connections. Crucial, not only for human development, but as a professional that is both influential and impactful.

This space has created opportunities that allow introverts to truly shine - but only if you're strategic. It's important that you take the time to foremost honor yourself and the boundaries you need. Likewise, you must also honor yourself by showing up fully in your calling.

Being an Influential Introvert means you must engage with people - that's the influential part. But you also must honor the way you show up - that's the introvert part.

Although I was clear on who I was and what I brought to the proverbial table, I was leaving pieces of myself strewn aside to uphold the expectations and perceptions of others, until one day there was hardly any of me left to give. Little by little, life began to stealthily creep onto my well-planned path like high tide at night until I was washed away into a new territory so unfamiliar, I didn't even recognize myself.

Some months after embarking upon my journey as a speaker and coach, I learned I was pregnant with a sneaky little rascal of a son. My decision to create my own path was solidified because I wanted to set an example for my kiddo that you can and must pursue your dreams and live your values.

My decision to fully pursue entrepreneurship wasn't easy. Traveling 90 minutes to 2 hours each way just to be able to take my son to daycare before heading to the corporate job that would fund my budding enterprise. Spending lunch hours meeting with potential clients, coaching current ones, honing my craft. Late nights collaborating with fellow entrepreneurs, creating curricula, writing and recording and refining.

Although I have a loving, supportive husband, I had to be strategic with both my time and my energy to create those opportunities for engagement. I had to decide what was most important to me and how I wanted to build upon that importance in each facet of my life, within the spaces that mattered.

My time with clients is necessary - being fully present supports the blossoming of their greatness in co-creation. My family time is central - whether for minutes or days, I'm fully present when with my boys or with my family of blood and bond. My Mommy time is sacred - for me to be my best, quiet time alone is essential to recharge and decompress. And my boys know well the truth of the saying "if mama ain't happy, ain't nobody happy".

It was non-negotiable for me to show my son, as well as my nieces and nephews, that your vision is important and acting toward it is in equal measure a right, a privilege, and a responsibility. Even if starting with baby steps, by honoring ourselves and the solutions we bring, we can honor others in service and love.

The influential are clear that a community is only as strong as the weakest member. They set themselves up for success by continuously working to do better and be better for themselves and their communities of influence. When you are clear about what you intrinsically offer and confident in the value your presence provides, you can joyously and lovingly serve others through your gifts, talents, quirks, abilities, and proficiencies. Playing to one's strengths opens space and opportunities for you to shine, as well as others.

FOOD FOR THOUGHT

I challenge you to integrate margins in your life to honor how you operate in the world:

- What are some pathways you can co-create to receive joy and balance?
- What consistent block of time can you carve out daily to share your solutions and invite people to your offerings?

Are you worthy of the truth of yourself? Or are you allowing your influence on your world to be diminished because you think that, as an introvert, you can't HAVE "those things"?

Your Joy Is Service

All of this has culminated into a new phase of truly embracing the Excitable Introvert that I am. Being an excitable introvert is one thing but stepping out and being branded as "The Excitable Introvert" - well, that's a whole 'nother something.

But what I've come to realize is that my joy - me showing up in my enthusiasm and in my excitement - is a service. It allows people to find themselves in my story, in my life, and in the lessons that I've learned.

As an excitable introvert, my joy gives my fellow introverts permission to be open and engaging, and to receive that which they most need. More than merely getting things bought and sold, my joy and openness facilitate connections, opportunities, and collaborations. As The Excitable Introvert, I provide my services and products in a way that no one else can.

Beyond my intellect and credentials, by intimately knowing what it's like to need that balanced ebb and flow between connecting with others in service and retreating into quiet, reflective solitude, I recreate that experience for my clients. It's through the act of being in honest seclusion and embracing one's embodied excitement that allows community to be built. My presence shifts atmospheres, especially when I allow my inward energy to be outward focused.

One of my greatest joys in this phase is cultivating a community of introverted women of color in business who are leading global shifts in their respective spaces. It's an honor and joy being able to gather these women and create a safe space where we don't have to justify our need to drop out sometimes, or why it's a struggle to pick up a phone.

Co-creating greatness generates magic that manifests influence and income steeped in honor, service, and love. We can be ourselves while generously and powerfully uphold one another to "show up, be awesome, and go home". We've connected and collaborated solutions amongst one another and our respective communities.

But without the realization that my joy is a service, none of this could have unfolded. Recognize that your joy and excitement are the secret sauce of your solution. The more sincere joy you share, all the more you can show up in your world to offer much needed, just-right solutions through loving service.

The influential have reason to rejoice because their wins are from the experiences of those they serve. They invest in themselves to see the harvest in others, knowing that there is surely a yield for every ordeal. This confident joy is a light of hope, possibility, and transformation that shapes the lives of all they impact for the better. Serving with joy allows you to amplify your impact well beyond the contract, conversation, or encounter.

FOOD FOR THOUGHT

I challenge you to consider how you can deliver your joy as service, so that your solution and your excitement about what you're offering becomes an answered prayer to those who would hire you, work for you, follow you, or champion you.

- How can you create an environment where your joy is at the center of what you deliver and how you deliver it?
- How can you show up in a way that gracefully honors you and your clients?

Are you expressing the truth of yourself? Or are you allowing your influence through your world to be diminished because you think that, as an introvert, you can't DO "those things"?

You Are an Influential Introvert

Being an introvert with influence is all about making an impact and an income while honoring your introverted nature. By seeing yourself truthfully, setting loving boundaries, and embodying joyful service, you create space to embrace your AWESOME. As you share your Amazing Works of Expression Serving Others with Maximum Enjoyment, you cause a ripple effect of transformation in your world.

While doing this is simple, it's not necessarily easy. Going from introvert to influential requires strategy and ongoing implementation. You owe it to yourself to be consistent, disciplined, and focused. Without it, you'll never reach the heights you were destined for and those who need you will never get the level of relief that only you and your solution can provide.

If you'd like to better leverage your introverted nature for income and impact with passion and purpose, I want you to know that there is a space for you. I invite you to join me for The Influential Introvert - a multi-faceted program specifically for introverted women of color.

Each lesson is designed to incrementally elevate you and your business with grace and ease. You'll discover the most important questions to ask yourself and your clients in order to make the most of your introversion. From there, you'll craft the just-right strategy that meets your needs for work, home, and beyond. Along the way, you will receive guidance from me and a community of women who understand your struggles and who will joyously triumph your wins. We recognize the need to honor the ebb and flow of loving service and quiet solitude and thus, balance structure and engagement to allow time for both being and doing.

I encourage you to join me at *www.TheInfluentialIntrovert.com* - and if you use the code **MATTER**, you'll get a little something extra to sweeten the deal.

Parting Is Sweet Sorrow

Allow me to share the story of one amazing young lady. She grew up painfully shy and introverted, always the quiet one on the side. But she had a passion to perform and routinely blew people away whenever so she dared open her mouth. Eventually, this duality became too much, and she knew she had to make a change to achieve her dreams. She decided to push her boundaries and to honor herself by serving with passion, love, and excellence.

She created an intentional version of herself - an empowered alter ego if you will. As she began to step more and more into her full potential, this meek, reserved young woman was able to create a platform that redefined cultures, shaped history, and made her one of the wealthiest people on the planet.

Through her successes and her struggles, she allowed her introverted nature to both inform and transform her life and the lives of those she impacted. She used her introspection and insight to give back and serve in every capacity she desires. She continues to inspire and empower women across the globe through her art, her presence, and her commitment to shared excellence.

This extraordinary introvert is known to most of us as Beyoncé.

Whenever you question whether you can be both influential and introverted, remember her story and find yourself in it. There are no limits to the ways that you can show up and influence as an introvert. You are already equipped and empowered - you need only to decide to receive all the good that comes from being an Influential Introvert.

Shining brightly as the powerful being you are, making bank and a bang within your own cozy space. And that's truly awesome.

About the Author

As "The Excitable Introvert", I guide introverted women of color to get seen, heard, and respected by embracing their AWESOME. When not jet setting, cracking wise, or hugging my son and his nine cousins, you can find me lurking online at *www.iEmbraceAwesome.com.*

* * *

To learn more by enrolling in Jacqueline's masterclass, point your cell phone's camera at the QR code then click the link:

MONIQUE S.
TOUSSAINT

Coach. Consultant. Cheerleader.

Monique S. Toussaint is the President of Monumental Business Solutions LLC where she creates an environment for leaders and business owners to identify strategies and create plans to achieve career and operational success. She invests time, passion and creativity into helping her clients explore and then implement solutions. This dynamic leader has over a decade of experience in strategic planning, program development and management; five years of coaching after earning the Global Career Development Facilitator credential; and is a natural supporter and cheerleader of others working towards achieving their goals. In this role, she serves as a continual thought partner, coach, speaker, and/or trainer for fellow business owners, colleagues and professionals. If you have an idea, she has a plan. It is her personal mission to see others succeed.

A firm believer in education, she holds a B.S. in Business Administration from the Kogod School of Business at American University in Washington, DC, a M.A. in Education and Human Development from George Washington University and received her Global Career Development Facilitator (GCDF) credential. A lifelong learner, she is a 2020-2021 Excellence in Government Fellow with the Partnership for Public Service and is also pursuing her doctorate in Organizational Change and Leadership at the University of Southern California.

A lady after God's heart, Monique serves on the Nurses Ministry, Silent Witnesses Mime Ministry, and Youth and Young Adult Encounter Bible Study Leadership Team at Greater Mount Calvary Holy Church in Washington DC. She is always ready to serve others, in life and in business.

CONTACT:

Website: www.monumentalbusiness.com

Email: Solutions@monumentalbusiness.com

Facebook: ***www.facebook.com/ThinkMonumental***

Instagram: *@ThinkMonumental*

MAKE YOUR *Moments* MATTER!

Maximizing Pivotal Opportunities to Shape your Leadership Journey

Leadership requires action. That's it. That's the premise for this chapter. If you do not get anything else from this chapter, walk away with the notion that you must act in order to impact change in your life and the lives of those destined to be touched by you. However, how you define what action to take is outlined in the next few pages. So, take some time and let's walk through what should entice you to act and implement change in your leadership journey.

When you think about leadership, there is a natural inclination to think about the business realm. You are encouraged to think beyond that. Leadership is multifaceted and can be viewed through various lens. Leaders exist in the home, marketplace, religious institutions, communities, and in everyday relationships. What is just as important as recognizing that you are a leader in the various areas of your life, is the understanding that the actions that you take as a leader often begin in your mind. Leadership is the compilation of moments that inform your experiences and the way you think and engage with the people around you. These critical moments in your life are the focus of the discussion. Identifying these moments, maximizing them, and evaluating how they contribute to your leadership journey is manifested in the following pages. The ultimate goal is to get you to appreciate the moments and make them matter.

To get us started, I will share one of my defining moments and how my use of the techniques discussed later helped me to make it matter.

Currently, as a senior leader of an office that did not exist when I began my leadership journey, I often reflect on the moments that brought me to where I am. These moments occurred at pivotal points in my career. Some have been in the face of adversity. Others were initiated because of leveraged resources and personal relationships. Regardless of the moment, there was always one opportunity that emerged when I was at the crossroads of comfort and progress. I would be lying to you if I said that the process of identifying the one moment that changed it all was not painful. The decision to leave what I was comfortable with was a hard one. Even in the face of adversity, there is the old adage about sticking with "the devil you know versus the devil you don't know."

Because of my decision to capitalize on a pivotal opportunity, I am now a better leader. I am more confident. I have garnered the respect of other senior leaders in my organization. I have made a positive impact on more people than I thought possible. I have leveraged resources to catapult programming that exceeded expectations, and many other things have transpired all because I chose to maximize one moment.

You may be thinking what does this mean for me? How do I maximize the moment? How do I maximize the opportunity?

Do I even know what either of these questions mean? Keep reading. You will see how the identification, application, and evaluation of maximizing pivotal opportunities in your life, help shape the journey you take as a leader.

Before we move forward, let's make sure that we are talking about the same thing. What really is a moment? Merriam-Webster defines a moment in at least seven different ways. For the purposes of this chapter, when we refer to a moment, we will be discussing "a comparatively brief period of time" that serves as "a stage in historical or logical development," and is "a cause or motive of action." Hopefully, by the end of the chapter, you will see your moment as "a time of excellence or conspicuousness." In summary, it should be clear what the defining times in your life were that led you to pursue a course of action in your leadership journey.

Identify the Moment

Now that you know what a moment is, it is essential for you to take a mental journey to identify your defining moments. Not all moments are life-changing and not all moments are critical to your leadership growth. My goal is to get you thinking about moments in your life that influenced the behaviors you currently demonstrate as a leader. So, grab a writing utensil and some paper or whatever electronic means you use to capture notes and get ready to carve out some time to do some exploratory, introspective work. Using the guiding questions below should help you identify your defining moments in your leadership journey.

First, take some time to reflect.

1. Can you readily identify moments that changed your life? If so, what was it about the moment(s) that stood out to you?
2. Did the moment impact your leadership journey? How has that moment impacted your growth as a leader?

3. Were there any relationships that pushed you to become a better leader? How? At what point in time did you notice the transition? Why was this relationship a factor in your leadership journey?
4. Is there a specific instance that signaled a change or adjustment in your leadership style?

Remember, your path to leadership may not have begun with your career, so I encourage you to keep an open mind in your moments of reflection. Was it that one time in elementary school when you were a member of safety patrol or recognized your level of influence as the class clown? Did something happen in high school when you were in a play or presenting a science project and discovered your ability to capture an audience with your presentation skills? Perhaps you were a college athlete and noticed that leadership was not based solely on popularity but a balance of hard work, commitment, and integrity. Was it the moment you held your child for the first time and you just knew you had to forge a path of success from that day forward? Whatever happened in your life up to this point contributed to who you are as a leader. The goal here is to help you recognize which moments did.

Next, acknowledge and recognize the defining moments for what they are.

1. What was it that made this moment stand out to you?
2. Were there immediate changes that you experienced because of this moment?
3. Did the moment make you laugh, cry, smile or become angry?
4. What can you deduce from the moment that contributed to your leadership growth?

These critical moments in our lives, once realized, can be a beacon of light for the future that we are building now. Your defining moment can be shaped by an experience with a leader that exhibited characteristics you want to emulate or never replicate. It may be a conversation you had with a grandparent who imparted some wisdom that you chose to apply in your behavior and efforts to lead others. It may be a meeting with a colleague, an encounter with a stranger, some tactics that you learned at a symposium, or an excerpt from a religious experience. Regardless of when you recognized the moment, it is important that you do. There is something empowering about identifying a defining moment in your life and being able to articulate it as such.

Then, recognition of your defining moments should prompt you to react.

1. What does this moment motivate you to do?
2. What is your plan of action for how you want to capitalize on this realized moment?
3. What are some intended consequences, positive or negative, if you react to this moment? How does your reaction impact others? How does your reaction impact your leadership journey?
4. Is it too late to react to this moment?

It is critical that you make a decision to act. To be clear, inaction is still an action. Whether you press pause or play on the television (TV) remote, you still are taking action. Both have consequences. One will make the TV enter a sleep mode eventually. Another will take you to the end of the current journey of what you were watching. Both times though, your decision to press pause or play will still generate an outcome. One allows you to see how things played out and the other prompts a delay in forward movement.

Maximizing the Moment

Leadership requires action. Just like with the TV, you have to decide how you want to handle your defining moments. Ignoring them does not change the fact that they happened.

Pivotal opportunities left ignored may result in regret later in life. I would recommend taking a chance and learning a lesson versus missing an opportunity that could have enhanced your life.

If you have taken the time to complete the necessary introspection above, you are already well on your way. You have identified your defining moments, recognized them as such, and now you are primed and ready to maximize the moment. How? Good question. To do this, you should set up a system that allows accountability, communication, and tailored responses (A.C.T.) to the moments that you have identified as defining ones. By deciding to A.C.T., it helps to ensure that you pivot in the direction you are destined to go in your leadership journey. Details pertaining to how to A.C.T. are below:

- Accountability
  - Find someone you trust and respect. Deciding to act on a moment realized and not sharing it with someone else allows you an escape route to inaction. Writing down your plan of action and keeping it to yourself is almost a guarantee to a delay or changed decision. When you articulate your desired plans with someone who you know will actually hold you accountable and not allow you to make excuses, you set yourself up for success. All cars have brakes, but they also have seat belts, air bags, and emergency brakes to help passengers in case of an accident. Nothing works well alone. Neither should you. Put a system of accountability in place to maximize your moment. It does not and should not be the same person for every defining moment. But create a support system that wants the best for you and is unashamed in pushing you to grow as a leader.

- Communication
    - Share your progress as you grow. Having an accountability system in place that you are not communicating with periodically is almost pointless. To set the moment up for success, you have to continually communicate with your system. The only way they will know if you are actually doing what you said you would do, is if you communicate. Set a scheduled time to communicate and then follow through on your meeting.
    - You should also share your growth with the people you lead and those around you. Your leadership journey does not affect you alone. In fact, it is more for the people around you than it is for you. Yes, you grow. Yes, you impact change. But a true reflection of your leadership is how you empower the people around you to grow as well.
- Tailored Responses
    - Evaluate growth and adjust along the way. You can maximize the moment best by pivoting in various situations when necessary. Very rarely is any journey a straight shot. You will encounter corners, turns, hills, valleys, bumps, etc. but what matters most is how you react when you encounter these things. Ideally, you do not want to take a turn unprepared and squeeze the person next to you in the car or run the car in the next lane off the road.
    - Success requires adjustment. Every response to your defining moment will not be the same. Different audiences, different situations, different moments in time will require you to respond differently. Take note of how your responses shift the environment and adjust how you respond as you grow.

It is never too late to grow. It is never too late to change. It is never too late to maximize a moment. You just need to focus on how you do it and do it well. Take the necessary steps to act.

Evaluating your Application

The work does not end because you have maximized the moment. This is a continual journey of growth as a leader. You rotate from a place of making decisions to having decisions made for you. How you react to those decisions matter. Being intentional about how you respond is instrumental to whether or not you pivot accordingly to maximize the moment.

When it is finished, you should once again reflect on how you maximized your moment. Are there are any things that you would have done differently? Are there any resources that you would have leveraged better? What does this moment mean for your future? Did you use it to grow? These are all questions to take into consideration regarding your defining moment.

Evaluating your response and planning to maximize the moment in the future is essential to continual growth. Sometimes life happens, perspectives change, the people involved change, but you and who you are as a leader may feel comfortable staying the same. Do yourself a favor. Don't. No one person should be the same person they woke up as ten years ago. Yes, leaders should be consistent. If that is the case, consistently evolve, consistently grow, and consistently commit to being a better leader every day.

Conclusion

Our lives begin to change the moment we decide to take a step in the direction of the future we want for ourselves. You have taken the time to maximize the moments that shape your leadership journey. Now that you have completed the introspective work to grow as a leader, you can walk away with the knowledge of what a moment is, how you identify it, apply it, and evaluate it. You should feel equipped to maximize pivotal opportunities. You now know that leadership requires you to A.C.T. accordingly. Adhering to a system with accountability, communication, and tailored responses is essential as you grow. Choosing not to act is also a decision. By deciding to act, you have chosen not to take the journey alone, and you know that the best way to continue to grow and maximize moments is to evaluate them and adjust accordingly. Remember everything that you experienced today and as you continue to grow as a leader, revisit the steps taken and repeat as necessary. Never forget that leadership requires action. Leadership takes work. Leadership takes time. Leadership is a compilation of moments realized. Define your moment. Own your moment. Maximize your moment.

Time To Act

After reading this chapter, you may be inclined to explore moments in your life that you may have overlooked. There may be an internal nudge to decide if there is a moment that you can tap into to shape your leadership journey. You may have already recognized your defining moment and want an opportunity to explore how to maximize it. If at any point of this chapter, you felt it in your gut that you wanted to dig deeper, I implore you not to ignore that feeling. Schedule a consultation with me at *https://calendly.com/thinkmonumental* and we can explore your moment together. Your journey is waiting on you to maximize your moment and pivot in the direction that will propel you as a leader. Do not deny yourself the opportunity to grow. Make your moment matter today.

* * *

To learn more by enrolling in Monique's masterclass, point your cell phone's camera at the QR code then click the link:

DR. CHERITA

WEATHERSPOON

Her purpose is clear, "Empowering you to be who you were created to be, to do the work you were called to do, and to live the life you desire to live." Through Spoonfed Motivation, LLC, Dr. Cherita Weatherspoon does just that.

Within her Powerhouse Coaching brand, Cherita works with professional Black women seeking to ignite their power, increase their impact, and accelerate their income through entrepreneurship as a coach, consultant, speaker, trainer, or author.

As a publisher, she is committed to empowering Black and Brown communities through the power of words. Her recent projects include the Women Who Launch & Lead Podcast, Love Letters to My Girls: 100+ Black Women Speak to the Hearts of Black Women & Girls, and Let Us Make A Man: The Black Man's Guide to Create A Life of Significance, Impact & Power.

Dr. Cherita, an international speaker and best-selling author, is a senior contributor for Women of More Magazine. She is also the founder of the BABE app which helps promote Black and Brown women experts and Mocha Tees, an apparel brand that celebrates Black women.

CONTACT:

Website: www.cheritaweatherspoon.com

Email: info@cheritaweatherspoon.com

To book a Power to Profit Discovery Call: *www.coachmedrc.com*

Facebook/Instagram/Twitter/Clubhouse: *@coachcherita*

LinkedIn: @DrCherita

MAKE YOUR *Business* MATTER!

Entrepreneurship seems to be a hot trend. So many people want to start a business. They are attracted to the allure of the six and seven-figure income streams. They crave time freedom. They dream of location freedom. They want the benefits of entrepreneurship but often fail to capitalize on the power of entrepreneurship. That is the power to make a difference–to build a business with impact.

As a business implementation strategist, I connect with a lot of people who are aspiring, emerging, or established entrepreneurs and I work specifically with professional Black women coaching them to launch six-figure expert businesses as coaches, consultants, speakers, trainers, and authors. I've heard a lot of different reasons why people start a business but they can all be boiled down to one of these two: they either want to make a difference or they want to make money. It's as if you have to choose between the two. I know from experience that you can do both, and I believe that you should do both. That's what I help my clients to do and that's what I want to help position you to do.

Many things can serve as the impetus for the launch of a business. For me, it was getting laid off from my executive leadership role at a university. However, I knew for years that I would launch a business before I actually did so. The layoff is what forced me to evaluate what I really wanted and what I was willing to do to get it. It forced me to face my fears. However, I often hear the same three reasons from people seeking my help to launch their business and while these reasons may seem like legitimate reasons, they often lead to serious problems in your business. When I hear these reasons, it puts me on high alert because I recognize how these three specific reasons can push people into businesses they hate or place them on a path leading to a downward spiral to failure.

The 3 Worst Reasons to Start A Business

Reason #1: I need the money

Starting a business solely because you need the money is setting yourself up for failure. People who make this mistake often seek business opportunities that promise quick or easy money. They are easily swayed by the promise of what is possible for them and miss what is required of them to make those possibilities a reality. They often give up easily when things get difficult and blame the "opportunity" for being the problem when they don't make the money they thought they would make. I've also noticed that people who are in business for themselves for the money only are more susceptible to doing whatever it takes to make money. That often means compromising their integrity and, at worst, endangering other people. Never start a business from a place of lack. It will cause you to make decisions that you otherwise would not make and behave in ways that you otherwise would not behave. Is money important? Absolutely! You can make plenty of it as a derivative of choosing to make a difference in the world rather than being singularly focused on making money because you need money. If money is what you ultimately desire, you will go wherever you think the money is and that can lead you into some dark and scary places, emotionally, spiritually, and perhaps physically.

Reason # 2: For my family or other people

This sounds like a noble reason to start a business, doesn't it? But the truth is that entrepreneurship is a significant undertaking that, at least in the early stages, can take a lot of time and resources to get off the ground and profitable. When you launch a business for someone other than yourself, you may face disappointment when they don't understand the amount of time it is taking away from them, or the resources it is taking from your home, or when they are generally not supporting you in the way you want them to. You can begin to feel resentment towards them because you are doing this for them and they don't appreciate it, or they don't understand what it takes to be successful.

Of course, you want your family to benefit from your work but when you're talking about why you are making the decision to start a business, you must have a deeper reason that sustains you than doing it for someone else. What is at the core of you doing it for your spouse, your parents, or your children? What is it that you want them to experience as a result and why? Why is that important to you? The answers to those questions are what will keep you focused when the people you are doing it for make you wonder why you're doing it.

Reason #3: I hate my job

This is another shallow reason for starting a business. It may be true, but hating your job is not a strong enough reason to pursue entrepreneurship. Starting a business may not resolve the real issues surrounding your feelings about your employment. You want to enter entrepreneurship with clarity of focus, determined intention, and a realistic perspective of what it is going to require of you. It is not a decision to be made based on your emotions. Starting a business has a lot in common with getting married. You want to enter in with your eyes wide open along with knowledge, patience, resilience, and compassion, among other things, recognizing that it won't be easy and being committed to stick with it and doing what it takes to make it work. If you start a business just to escape a bad situation, you could find yourself in another bad situation because it was never the situation you were supposed to be in.

You can easily see how these reasons lack focus on doing work that matters, and while it may seem like it's not that important–work is work and business is business–the truth is, the work matters. What you do matters. Why you do it matters. And, when you figure that out, life–and work and business–becomes much more fulfilling.

When I lost my job, I didn't immediately jump into my business. I took the time to figure out if it was something I was ready to do and could be committed to for the long term. I weighed the pros and cons. I prayed. I sought counsel from people I could trust to respond to me based on my situation and desires, and not their situation, fears, or mistakes. I recognized the seriousness of the decision and weighed my options carefully over a couple of months before making the decision to start my business. I was intentional in the launch of my business and I am intentional in the work I do in my business because I recognized that I wanted to do work that mattered.

Intention, Impact, and Income

There are several words used to convey the same concept. Aim, mission, purpose, intention. They all speak to what you mean to do and imply that there is a level of commitment attached to whatever that aim, mission, purpose, or intention is. It is the setting of a course of action and then taking action. An intention, or whichever variance of the word you prefer, is nothing without the definitive action that follows it. If you mean to do it, then you take action to do it; otherwise, your intention is not much more than a dream or a wish.

Impact, which can be either a noun or a verb, is about connection. It can be described as what occurs when someone or something comes forcibly into contact with someone or something else (noun) or to have a strong effect on someone or something (verb). When it comes to business, unless you are intentional about having a positive impact on those you serve, you can very easily have a negative impact or no impact at all. And when you are intentional, you can find yourself being thrust into contact with the people who need you and your solution most. If you are not intentional about building a business with impact, you can find yourself feeling like your work doesn't matter, feeling unfulfilled, resentful, and ready to give up. But it doesn't have to be that way.

You can have a business that is impactful for your clients and that brings you joy but it requires intention.

I mentioned earlier that it seems as if people believe you have to choose between making money and making a difference. Something I hear quite often from people who believe the work they are called to do is aligned with their God-given purpose is that they don't think they should get paid for doing their work or that they shouldn't get paid well for doing their work. I know without a doubt that the work I do in my business is aligned with the work God called me to do in the world. I also know without a doubt that prosperity and abundance are a part of His plan for my life and that my business is just one of the ways I can experience those things.

Sidebar: If you struggle in this area, download my *31 Scriptures for Black Women Entrepreneurs* to help you lean in and align with how God sees you and what He desires for you. You can find it at *www.powerhouseyou.com/31-scriptures*.

If you want to make an impact but not make money, you can accomplish that easily. However, if you desire to build a business that makes an impact while making you a significant income, you have to be intentional about it. It can be done with simplicity and ease, but not without intention.

Build A Business with Impact

What does it mean to build a business with impact? It means that you are intentional in how you design your business so that it serves you well while it is also serving your clients or customers well. It means that you step into the role of CEO from the beginning stages of your business rather than operating with an employee mindset and displaying employee behavior. Building a business with IMPACT means that you look ahead to the future and determine what you want to experience and then lay the foundation from the beginning that will support the manifestation of that vision. It also means that while you recognize the importance of transactions in your business, you focus on delivering products and services that allow your clients or customers to experience a transformation, knowing that the more transformative your work is, the more transactions your business will have.

Your mindset shifts from:

Transactions > Transformation to

Transformation = Transactions

When you are solely focused on transactions, your primary considerations are money, revenue, sales, and expenses. You are more concerned with what is coming into your business than you are with what your business is putting out into the world. When you attain a better balance between transactions and transformation, you are equally concerned about impact, fulfillment, passion, and purpose and how those things translate into transactions (money, revenue, sales, expenses). They are both important and your business can be transformational for your clients or customers, and for you.

Let me be transparent and share that when I first launched my business, I didn't know this. And, none of the coaches I invested in told me. It was all about the fastest path to cash. I followed that path for several months but quickly figured out that it wasn't the path for me. After some trial and error, launching and relaunching, and finally asking myself some important questions about the work I was doing and the work I wanted to do, I got the clarity I needed to launch the business that brings me both joy and profit. Out of that experience was born the IMPACT Framework™. It's the process I take my clients through to ensure they design a business that is meaningful to them and those they serve before spending the time and money to build and launch that business.

The IMPACT Framework™

My proprietary IMPACT framework is defined by six pillars that are essential to building a solid foundation for a business that serves you and those you serve. The six pillars are Intent, Mission, Power, A-Game, Change Process, and Transformation. Here's a brief overview of each pillar:

Intent - This pillar is focused on getting clear on your why. It's divided into two components, the internal and external. The internal why digs deep into the root of why you are choosing entrepreneurship as your path. The external why focuses on those who will be impacted by your work.

Mission - This pillar is focused on answering the what question. It helps you identify what you want to do in your business and what you want to accomplish through your business.

Power - In the Power pillar, you identify what sets you apart from others in the marketplace who do similar work to what you plan to do.

A-Game - This pillar helps you identify how you specifically make a difference and deliver results for those you serve.

Change Process - In this pillar, you bring together the details of your intent, mission, power, and A-Game to develop the specific process you will implement with the people or organizations you serve to deliver the result you promise.

Transformation - In this last pillar, you get crystal clear on the transformation your results lead to through your work.

Being able to clearly and concisely answer the questions related to each of these pillars is the starting point to designing a business with impact that also delivers the income and independence you desire. Once the foundation has been laid, you can move on to building and launching the business that pays you well for the impact, results, and transformation you deliver.

This is what we do at Powerhouse Coaching. If you are ready to build a business with impact, learn more at *powerhouseyou.com/applyforimpact*.

* * *

To learn more by enrolling in Dr. Cherita's masterclass, point your cell phone's camera at the QR code then click the link:

DR. ROBERTA WILBURN

Dr. Roberta J. Wilburn is an award-winning diversity and inclusion expert who champions diversity, equity, and inclusion while inviting people to enhance their intercultural skills and build authentic relationships with people from diverse backgrounds in order to promote cross-cultural understanding. She is an author, diversity trainer, cultural coach, and racial justice advocate that works with people who are serious about uncovering their hidden biases and doing the necessary work to become culturally sensitive and responsive advocates and allies. Using her R.E.A.L. Diversity, Equity, and Inclusion Framework she teaches and encourages others how to embrace cultural differences and foster collaborative relationships with people from diverse backgrounds using a faith-based perspective so they can excel in a diverse and inclusive world.

As a transformational servant-leader, she has always tried to have her hands on the pulse of local and national concerns, and it has been recognized by others locally and nationally. In the fall of 2016, her diversity work was validated when she became the recipient of the *YWCA Women of Achievement Carl Maxey Racial and Social Justice Award and the following year, she received the 2017 Insight Into Diversity Giving Back Award for Administrators in Higher Education.* Her research has led her to pursue and acquire two international grants spanning Africa, Mexico, and the Dominican Republic; receive two invitations to present her research on women of color at the Oxford Round Table in England; and write numerous publications.

CONTACT:

Website: www.wilburnassociates.org

Instagram: *@wilburnassociatesllc*

Facebook/LinkedIn: *@robertawilburn*

Twitter: *@DrRWilburn*

MAKE YOUR *Inclusion* MATTER!

Make Diversity, Equity, Inclusion and Racial Justice Matter: Going Beyond a Slogan

"Race has always mattered in the United States,
at both societal and individual levels."
~ Brenda Allen (2011)

This Current Moment in History

Issues of diversity, equity and inclusion are real. Those of us who have been traditionally marginalized know only too well how real it is. It is not something we can deny or hide from. It is not something we can escape or pretend that it doesn't exist. Its impact is not something that can be reduced to a hashtag or slogan. Mary-Francis Winters (2020) describes in her book the real significance these experiences can have on Black people, in terms of what she calls "Black fatigue." She says that it is "the fatigue that comes from the pain and anguish of living with racism every single day of your life. It is about being fatigued by those who are surprised and express outrage (with no action) that such inequities still exist. It is about the constant fatigue of not knowing whether you or a loved [one] will come home alive. It is about enduring the ravages of intergenerational racism." While race has always mattered in the United States as Brenda Allen stated, racial justice has not. This has been the fundamental problem in our country throughout its history. It has made living in America while Black a lifelong challenge.

According to Elwood Watson, Black lives are continually being demeaned, devalued and dehumanized in the following ways:

"Driving while Black. Walking while Black, Running while Black. Sitting in a public space while Black. Asking for help while Black. Eating while Black. Merely existing while Black. The cold, hard truth is that to be Black in America is to frequently endure an ongoing state of assaults and insults. Indeed, it seems that being Black is synonymous with being under unrelenting emotional and psychological siege."

Nevertheless, Black people are resilient and are survivors. For those who survived the middle passage from Africa to the Americas had to be strong. Those who withstood the hardship of slavery, watching their families ripped apart, watching family members raped, beaten and lynched had to be strong. A people who endured the Jim Crow laws, being abused and discriminated against for centuries, and now facing racial profiling, wrongful incarceration and the onslaught of police brutality is too much for even the most resilient to bear indefinitely. So we have reached the perfect storm. COVD-19, a global pandemic, causing Black people to die at disproportionately alarming rates due to the impact of years of systemic racism that has caused health disparities in this country. Then we, as a people, had to endure the pain of back-to-back deaths of Ahmaud Arbery, the shooting of Briana Taylor in her own home, and repeatedly watching police officer with his knee on George Floyd's neck for 8 minutes and 46 seconds as he calls out for his mother until every breath was taken from his life. The never-ending list that goes on and on and it's just too much to bear. Then to see the peaceful protests turn to riots, looters stealing—marring the death of Floyd and the purpose of the marches and protests, the social media rants, the non-stop news highlighting militarized police, yet the police are repeatedly excused and never held accountable for killing unarmed Black people.

For a period after George Floyd's murder, Black Lives Matter (BLM) protests were not only taking place all over this nation, but also all over the world. Yet, as it always does, the protests dissipated, and the issues once again were pushed to the back of people's minds. Then business as usual ensued, and once again, there was a resurgence of killings of Black bodies with no real action or consequences. Making matters worse, White supremacists who stormed the Capitol are allowed to wreak havoc in Congress with the help of insiders, five people were killed, and virtually nothing was done. We all know that if this had been a Black Lives Matter protest, things would have been a lot different and not in a positive way. This is too hard to stomach!

My Reality Growing Up Black

I grew up in Brooklyn, New York in the sixties and as a child I believed that the racial injustices and discrimination my father told me about was a thing of the past. It wasn't my reality because I lived a very happy life interacting with children from various races. I even remember that my best friend in first grade was a white boy named AJ. I also remember a Hawaiian teacher who taught us dance. I clearly saw and recognized the differences in races, but it was insignificant to me. I was taught that New York with the Statue of Liberty in Ellis Island, standing as a prominent symbol of freedom and landmark, was a melting pot of diverse people and we were all Americans. That's all that mattered---that is, until I had to be bused across town to the all-white school as a result of forced integration.

Being bused for me was not what most people picture when they think of children and busing. I didn't have the privilege of taking a typical yellow school bus to get me across town; I had to learn to ride two city buses and take a subway train to get to my school when I was only 11 years old. Since my father worked full time like most of the other Black parents, he could not afford to take me to school every day. On the weekend before the start of the school year, my dad took me on a ride to show me what route I was supposed to take and then I was on my own. Fortunately, there were several other neighborhood children who were in the same predicament I was, so we traveled to school together. It was on one of these trips to school that I had my first encounter with racism.

The Ugly Realities of Racism

The subway train was the last leg of my morning ride to the school that I was integrating. It was standard practice for those of us traveling from my inner-city neighborhood in Brooklyn, after getting off the train, to stop at the newspaper stand to buy candy and other snacks to take to school. One morning as I was standing in line, waiting to pay for my goodies, and elderly white women dropped her change. Instinctually, I bent down to pick it up and hand it to her. I was taught by my parents to always respect my elders and to help them whenever possible. You can imagine how devastated I was when she turned around and started yelling at me. Calling me the "N" word and everything else except a child of God. I was hurt, embarrassed and being the emotional child that I was, I was left in tears. I'm sure I cried all the way to school. I don't remember what happened to the other children. They may have scattered when the woman started yelling at me. All I can remember is being alone to drown in my personal sorrows. When I got to school, I had to suck up my tears and get it together so I could do my work. There was no school counselor for me to talk to...no one for me to confide in. As a result, I carried this unresolved trauma through my tweens, to adolescences, and into adulthood. It is still very real to me today over fifty years later.

My husband, who grew up in the South in Arkansas, carries with him his own racialized traumatic childhood experiences that were even more horrific than what I experienced. These are not isolated experiences but are more typical than rare for People of Color. These are classic examples of racial trauma. According to Erica Hayes, "racial trauma is defined as the physical and psychological responses to cumulative or stressful experiences of racism. Like other traumas, Black, Indigenous and People of Color (BIPOC) who have experienced racism may develop hyper-vigilance, insomnia, anxiety, depressed mood, guilt, memory impairment, and self-blame." These are just some of the reasons why issues of diversity, equity, inclusion, and racial justice matter and why I became a champion for social justice.

Slogans Are Great, But We Need Much More

The Black Lives Matter (BLM) movement, which developed as a result of the death of 17-year-old Trayvon Martin who was walking home from the store with nothing but a bag of Skittles in his hand, reminds me of the "Say It Loud I'm Black and I'm Proud" slogan that gained momentum after the assassination of Dr. Martin Luther King. The slogan back then served as a catalyst to bring people together for a common cause. It was to channel the angry and negative energy into positive action. It was about changing feelings of being devalued by the American society into Black pride. While it did serve to boost the self-esteem of Black people, it did little to change the way the larger American society view Black people, nor did it lessen the violence and discrimination targeted toward us. While slogans are great to galvanize the support of people, it is not enough by itself to bring about long-term change. This too has that been the case of the BLM movement. While it seemed like this time, after the death of George Floyd, that things would be different, the brutality of his death seemed to cause a national awakening not only for in his community, but around the nation and the world. Those who had been questioning Black people, asking them "Why can't we just get over it?" or "Why do we always have to play the race card?" for the first time got a real glimpse into our world and why we have been crying out saying BLACK LIVES MATTER! However, the momentum was short lived because we must go beyond a slogan if we are going to get real about the issues of diversity, equity, inclusion, and racial justice.

The Illusion of Commitment: Optical Allyship and Performative Activism

There are some things we can't ignore. Racism is one of them. If you ignore the realities of racism, you are actively participating in perpetuating its continued existence. However, optical allyship and performative activism is not adequate. Both terms refer to the illusion of commitment to supporting the Black Lives Matter movement and other diversity, equity, and inclusion efforts. They are activities which on the surface seem to be supportive as Latham Thomas defines the concept: "... it makes a statement but does not go beneath the surface and is not aimed at breaking away from the systems of power that oppress."

As someone who purports to be a champion for diversity and social justice, I could not stand idly by without trying to do something to address the problems that I see in our country regarding race and promote greater understanding between people in this country. As individuals, we often question what we can do to make a difference in addressing a major problem like systemic racism. It is important for us to realize that no one can do everything. But if each one of us would exam what we can do within our own personal sphere of influence with the skills that God has given us, we can begin to eradicate many of challenges we see so prevalent in our country. Consider your sphere of influence and provide the greatest impact where you are with what you have.

Following the deaths of George Floyd and Brionna Taylor, there was an acceleration of activities to implement Diversity, Equity, and Inclusion (DEI) programs across corporate America, as well in higher education and other businesses and organizations. However, in many cases, these activities were performative and were solely done for the purpose of optics instead of any real commitment to diversity and social justice. For there to be lasting change, we have to take steps to actualize our commitment to diversity. That is why I developed my *R.E.A.L. Diversity, Equity and Inclusion (DEI) Framework.*

The terms diversity, equity, and inclusion have become common buzz words in many arenas. However, there are still people who have no idea what we are talking about or what the distinction is between the terms.

Diversity is the full breath of human differences, not just race. When you think of all the many ways that people are different, those are all components of diversity.

Equity is about everyone being treated fairly. Equity isn't necessarily equivalent to equality. Equality is about everyone getting the same thing. However, equality is meaningless unless we first ensure that there is equity. Equity is about making sure that everyone has what they need so they can have a fair chance at achieving success. In some cases, in order to achieve equity, some people will have to get more than others. For example, a tall person may be able to get an apple off of a tree just by reaching his hand straight up in the air. On the other hand, a short person can stand on her tiptoes and still not be able to get the apple. For the short person to have access to the apple, she will need to get a stool or a ladder. Equity is about leveling the playing field for those who may be at some type of disadvantage. Once the playing field has been leveled, then we can talk about giving everyone the same thing. That's equality.

Inclusion is making everyone feel welcomed and a part of the community regardless of whether it is at school, at work, or in the greater community at large. It is allowing people to use their gifts to the greatest extent possible to positively impact the whole group. It has been said that inclusion is not only inviting people to the dance but also making sure that they have an opportunity to dance once they get there.

Getting R.E.A.L. About Diversity, Equity, & Inclusion

I believe in building real, authentic relationships between diverse groups of people in order to build cross-cultural understanding. That is why I have been able to be successful in developing an array of cross-cultural relationships and learn to interact effectively across cultural groups. From these experiences, I conceptualized and developed my R.E.A.L. Diversity, Equity & Inclusion (DEI) Framework. It is based on the components I believe are necessary to help people who seriously want to move beyond just holding a sign that says Black Lives Matter and performative activism so they can get real about diversity, equity, and inclusion. R.E.A.L. is an acronym that stands for these essential components:

R- Relationships, Reflections, & Responsiveness

E- Education, Engagement, & Empowerment

A- Authenticity, Assessment, & Actualization

L- Lived Experiences, Lifelong Process, & Lifestyle of Diversity and Social Justice

The following is an infographic of the *R.E.A.L. DEI Framework:*

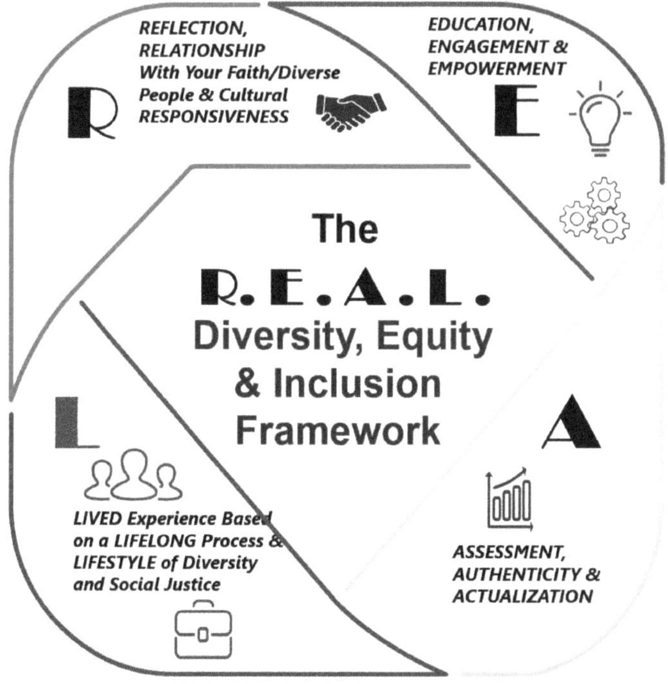

R.E.A.L. Diversity, Equity, & Inclusion (DEI) Framework

R - Relationships are key in becoming a culturally responsive and sensitive person who can work effectively with others from diverse backgrounds. However, it starts with you and your ability to self-reflect. Before you can consider having a relationship with someone else, you must have a firm grasp of who you are. It involves reflection of your relationship with your faith. Your faith helps you become grounded in your beliefs and values and gives you your moral compass. Once you are aware of how your belief system influences your actions, then you need to establish your relationships with diverse individuals with various social identity groups. Reflection is a key piece along the way. The following quotes describe the importance of reflection:

"Why Reflect? It is the language of reflection that deepens our knowledge of who we are in relation to others...."
Carole Miller & Juliana Saxton

"People who have had little self-reflection live life in a huge reality blind spot."
Bryant McGill

"Reflective thinking turns experience into insight."
John C. Maxwell

Reflection gives us insight on how to be responsive to others. In just about every culture, there is some form of the Golden Rule which says we should: "Do unto others as you would have them do unto you." However, if we take time to reflect and get to know people, we will learn how to apply the Platinum Rule: "Treat others the way they want to be treated." Just because you want to be treated a certain way doesn't necessarily mean that another person wants to be treated that way too, especially if they are from a different culture.

We need to create heart and soul connections with people who are different from us because it is often in the depths of the soul where we find our commonalities. Each person has a unique value. We should not characterize that uniqueness as bad simply because it is not a reflection of ourselves. We need to learn to unearth the beauty of the things that make us different so we can begin to appreciate each other.

E - Education, Engagement, and Empowerment are critical elements in the model. It is important that you do your own work in these areas. In order to be effective in addressing issues of diversity, equity, and inclusion, you have to your knowledge through personal development that addresses your blind spots and other areas that you need to develop. You also must engage in cultural activities and interact with groups from diverse cultural backgrounds. By doing these things, you can become empowered to be more effective in increasing cross-cultural understanding and associations.

A - Authenticity is about being open, transparent, and humble. Authenticity is important in building trust with others from diverse social identities. However, it is also important to apply the same authenticity that you use with others to yourself. Diversity and inclusion are built on authentic relationships. I need to be real with you so you can be real with me. Assessment helps to reveal where we are on our cultural awareness journey, so we know the next steps we need to take. It also helps to reveal implicit biases and blind spots you may be unaware you have. Once you have identified the areas where you need to further develop and you have done the work to address them, you will be in a position where you will be able to actualize your commitment to diversity, equity, and inclusion.

L - Since diversity and social justice are critical to our society, it is critical that each of us begins to accrue lived experiences in this area. These experiences should be based on a lifelong process of building a lifestyle of diversity, equity, and inclusion. Diversity and cultural awareness a lifelong journey, not a destination. It is not a one and done process. You can't take one course or have one Black friend and think you've achieved cultural competence. It is a lifelong process, and it needs to be incorporated as a regular part of your lifestyle.

Don't Wait to Have an Impact and Leave a Legacy

Each day, we have an opportunity to push pass our obstacles and move toward greatness. If we are going to make a difference in this world and create a life of unforgettable impact, we must be willing to get out of our comfort zone, look beyond our temporary discomfort, and be determined to leave a legacy for our family and the world. It is about striving for continued excellence. We can't become satisfied with the status quo. As an administrator, one of the things that I have always told my staff is if we are excellent today and we don't change anything we do, we will be mediocre tomorrow. As a result, my teams and I have been able to develop cutting edge programs and have remained relevant when other graduate programs were struggling.

You don't always know the level of impact that you have, but you have to continually strive to do your best. In January of 2017, I received the *Insight into Diversity Giving Back Award for Administrators in Higher Education.* This award is the only national award that honors college and university administrators for their commitment to diversity through leadership, and for giving back to their campus and community. I was very honored to receive this national award, but it was nothing compared to how I felt when I received a plaque upon my retirement in December of 2020 with numerous testimonials from not only my colleagues in the Whitworth University School of Education, but also from the President of the University and individuals with whom I had worked in the past. The following is just one of the many comments that I received:

"You are a committed, knowledgeable, engaged, and passionate colleague in advocating for diversity, equity, and inclusion. Through your leadership and activism at the university level as well as in the community and beyond, you have certainly advanced the understanding of what it means to be a culturally responsive educator and community member. Thanks for your faithfulness to move us to learn more about and resist racism and promote equity." Dr. David Cherry.

I didn't realize what an impact I had on so many people. I would love to help you learn how to have a lasting impact by enhancing your ability to excel in a diverse and inclusive world. This may seem intimidating, but when you feel like you have challenges that you are having problems tackling, don't be afraid to reach out to others for the help and support you need. Asking for help is not a sign of weakness, but a sign that you recognize your humanness. I realize that many people are serious about wanting to become more culturally proficient when they interact with people from diverse groups, but they don't know how. Change takes time. I invite you to make a commitment and invest in yourself by joining my year-long *Get R.E.A.L. Diversity Mastermind Program* based on my framework. Over a course of a year, you will work with me and others who are willing to put in the work like you to create lasting change for themselves and others. This is for people who are serious about moving beyond a slogan and performative activism in order to take a deep dive into diversity in a way that will make a R.E.A.L. difference.

* * *

To learn more by enrolling in Dr. Roberta's masterclass, point your cell phone's camera at the QR code then click the link:

CONCLUSION

"IT AIN'T OVER!"

So, in conclusion, as the great Urban Psalmist from the land of Harlem, USA, Teddy Riley once said, "It ain't over. It ain't over!"

That's right. This is not the end. It's just the beginning. While the pages in this book have ended, the journey to creating your life of unforgettable impact and abundant fulfillment is just getting started.

There is so much more to do! But the choice of if you're going to do it falls solely in your lap. We have done our part. We have given you this book, an online masterclass, a podcast, live and virtual events, video interviews, and even a feature film to advance the conversation and transformation beyond these pages. The rest is up to you.

Don't stop now. You've come too far. Make the commitment to living a life that matters and helping everyone around you do the same. Tell a friend to tell a friend about this project. Shout out @themakeitmatterproject on your social media. With your help, this project can reach heights greater than any of us could imagine. I look forward to continuing our work together and as one of our most prolific fallen street griots, Nipsey Hussle said, "We gonna do it real big."

Make It Matter!

MAKE IT MATTER!
Workbook

Ryan C. Greene

MAKE IT MATTER

My top takeaways are:

___

___

___

The areas in my life I plan to implement these teachings are:

___

___

___

I would like to work with Ryan in these ways:

___

___

___

Note from the *Make It Matter!* online masterclass module:

Linda Buckley

MAKE YOUR WORDS MATTER

My top takeaways are:

____

____

____

The areas in my life I plan to implement these teachings are:

____

____

____

I would like to work with Linda in these ways:

____

____

____

Note from the *Make It Matter!* online masterclass module:

Gregory Carter

MAKE YOUR MONEY MATTER

My top takeaways are:

___

___

___

The areas in my life I plan to implement these teachings are:

___

___

___

I would like to work with Gregory in these ways:

___

___

___

Note from the *Make It Matter!* online masterclass module:

Dr. Ashley Dash

MAKE YOUR LEGACY MATTER

My top takeaways are:

___

___

___

The areas in my life I plan to implement these teachings are:

___

___

___

I would like to work with Dr. Ashley in these ways:

___

___

___

Note from the *Make It Matter!* online masterclass module:

Mattie Deed

MAKE YOUR CREDIT MATTER

My top takeaways are:

____

____

____

The areas in my life I plan to implement these teachings are:

____

____

____

I would like to work with Mattie in these ways:

____

____

____

Note from the *Make It Matter!* online masterclass module:

Rev. Roger Dixon, Jr.

MAKE YOUR SUCCESS MATTER

My top takeaways are:

____

____

____

The areas in my life I plan to implement these teachings are:

____

____

____

I would like to work with Roger in these ways:

____

____

____

Note from the *Make It Matter!* online masterclass module:

Dr. Katrina Ferguson

MAKE YOUR WHY MATTER

My top takeaways are:

___

___

___

The areas in my life I plan to implement these teachings are:

___

___

___

I would like to work with Dr. Katrina in these ways:

___

___

___

Note from the *Make It Matter!* online masterclass module:

Juanita H. Grant

MAKE YOUR PARENTING MATTER

My top takeaways are:

____

____

____

The areas in my life I plan to implement these teachings are:

____

____

____

I would like to work with Juanita in these ways:

____

____

____

Note from the *Make It Matter!* online masterclass module:

Dr. Jonas Gadson, DTM

MAKE YOUR FUTURE MATTER

My top takeaways are:

____

____

____

The areas in my life I plan to implement these teachings are:

____

____

____

I would like to work with Dr. Jonas in these ways:

____

____

____

Note from the *Make It Matter!* online masterclass module:

Kimmoly K. LaBoo

MAKE YOUR STORY MATTER

My top takeaways are:

____

____

____

The areas in my life I plan to implement these teachings are:

____

____

____

I would like to work with Kimmoly in these ways:

____

____

____

Note from the *Make It Matter!* online masterclass module:

Brian J. Olds

MAKE YOUR MESSAGE MATTER

My top takeaways are:

____

____

____

The areas in my life I plan to implement these teachings are:

____

____

____

I would like to work with Brian in these ways:

____

____

____

Note from the *Make It Matter!* online masterclass module:

Suzanne Peters

MAKE YOUR PAIN MATTER

My top takeaways are:

___

___

___

The areas in my life I plan to implement these teachings are:

___

___

___

I would like to work with Suzanne in these ways:

___

___

___

Note from the *Make It Matter!* online masterclass module:

Mike Powell

MAKE YOUR GOALS MATTER

My top takeaways are:

____

____

____

The areas in my life I plan to implement these teachings are:

____

____

____

I would like to work with Mike in these ways:

____

____

____

Note from the *Make It Matter!* online masterclass module:

Jacqueline Shaulis

MAKE YOUR AWESOME MATTER

My top takeaways are:

____

____

____

The areas in my life I plan to implement these teachings are:

____

____

____

I would like to work with Jacqueline in these ways:

____

____

____

Note from the *Make It Matter!* online masterclass module:

Monique S. Toussaint

MAKE YOUR MOMENTS MATTER

My top takeaways are:

____

____

____

The areas in my life I plan to implement these teachings are:

____

____

____

I would like to work with Monique in these ways:

____

____

____

Note from the *Make It Matter!* online masterclass module:

Cherita Weatherspoon

MAKE YOUR WORK MATTER

My top takeaways are:

____

____

____

The areas in my life I plan to implement these teachings are:

____

____

____

I would like to work with Dr. Cherita in these ways:

____

____

____

Note from the *Make It Matter!* online masterclass module:

Dr. Roberta Wilburn

MAKE YOUR INCLUSION MATTER

My top takeaways are:

____

____

____

The areas in my life I plan to implement these teachings are:

____

____

____

I would like to work with Dr. Roberta in these ways:

____

____

____

Note from the *Make It Matter!* online masterclass module:

BONUS

Resources

MORE THAN JUST A BOOK...

Take advantage of all the

MAKE IT MATTER! resources...

Enroll in the online masterclass for deeper systematic contributor trainings, author interviews, featured spotlights, and other resources.

www.themakeitmatterproject.com/course

Subscribe to the ***MAKE IT MATTER!*** podcast and grow on the go with featured interviews of top leaders and influencers!

www.themakeitmatterproject.com/podcast

FREE WEBINAR

How To
MONETIZE YOUR EXPERTISE & GET PAID FOR WHAT YOU KNOW

TEXT PASSION TO (614) 333-0338 FOR INSTANT ACCESS

Register for one of Ryan's free webinars...

FREE WEBINAR

The Secrets to
BECOMING A TOP EARNING INDIE AUTHOR
(Without Being Famous)

TEXT AUTHOR TO (614) 333-0338 FOR INSTANT ACCESS

It's never too late to RESET. Catch every moment from this game changing event that was the pre-cursor to the Make It Matter! Project.

CATCH THE REPLAY OF THE MOST IMPACTFUL EVENT OF 2020.

On July 1, we hit the RESET Button on 2020! Don't miss your chance to write your greatest second act ever!
Register now for this free live virtual event.

SUMMIT HOST: RYAN C. GREENE

RESET YOUR MIND, LIFE, AND BUSINESS

FEATURING

MARC CLARKE | DR. CHERYL WOOD | STEPHEN HILL | TIANA PATRICE | DR. DONALD GRANT JR. | KEARN CHERRY | DR. ANGELA CUDGER | MIKE POWELL | DR. KATRINA FERGUSON | BROOKE-SIDNEY J. HARBOUR

WATCH THE REPLAY: HTTP://BIT.LY/RESET2020REPLAY

A special thank you goes to our sponsors.
Please support their business.

Kearn Cherry
PRN Home Care & Power Up Summit

www.prnhomecareservices.com
www.powerupsummit
https://www.linkedin.com/in/kearncherry
Facebook: @kearn.crockettcherry
Instagram: @kearncherry
Twitter: @KearnCherryPRN

Dr. Catherine Johnson
Optimal Neuroholistic Services

www.DrCatherineJackson.com
Instagram: @DrCatherineJackson
Twitter: @DrCCJackson
Facebook: Dr.Catherine.Jackson

CPSIA information can be obtained
at www.ICGtesting.com
Printed in the USA
BVHW091323150321
602076BV00005B/41/J